Paris

Julian Green was born to American parents in Paris in 1900 and spent most of his extraordinary literary career there, writing in French for a wide European readership. He published over sixty-five books in France, including novels, essays, plays and many volumes of his journal. In addition, he published five celebrated books in the United States. During the First World War, Green served in the American Red Cross and then in the French Army; during the Second World War, he worked at the US Office of War Information, broadcasting to France on the radio. As an American, he gained the honour of being the only foreign member of the Académie Française. He died in Paris in 1998.

Lila Azam Zanganeh was born in Paris in 1976. She has taught literature, cinema and Romance languages at Harvard University and now writes and lives mainly in New York City. Her book *The Enchanter: Nabokov and Happiness* was published by Allen Lane in 2011.

JULIAN GREEN

Paris

*Bilingual edition with an English translation
by* J. A. UNDERWOOD
and with an Introduction by LILA AZAM ZANGANEH
Photographs by JULIAN GREEN

PENGUIN BOOKS

PENGUIN MODERN CLASSICS

Published by the Penguin Group
Penguin Books Ltd, 80 Strand, London WC2R ORL, England
Penguin Group (USA) Inc., 375 Hudson Street, New York, New York 10014, USA
Penguin Group (Canada), 90 Eglinton Avenue East, Suite 700, Toronto, Ontario, Canada M4P 2Y3
    (a division of Pearson Penguin Canada Inc.)
Penguin Ireland, 25 St Stephen's Green, Dublin 2, Ireland (a division of Penguin Books Ltd)
Penguin Group (Australia), 250 Camberwell Road, Camberwell, Victoria 3124, Australia
    (a division of Pearson Australia Group Pty Ltd)
Penguin Books India Pvt Ltd, 11 Community Centre, Panchsheel Park, New Delhi – 110 017, India
Penguin Group (NZ), 67 Apollo Drive, Rosedale, Auckland 0632, New Zealand
    (a division of Pearson New Zealand Ltd)
Penguin Books (South Africa) (Pty) Ltd, 24 Sturdee Avenue, Rosebank, Johannesburg 2196, South Africa

Penguin Books Ltd, Registered Offices: 80 Strand, London WC2R ORL, England

www.penguin.com

First published in France by Champ Vallon 1983
Republished in France by Editions du Seuil 1989
This translation first published in Great Britain and the United States of America
    by Marion Boyars Publishers Ltd 1991
This edition published in Penguin Classics 2012

003

Copyright © Champ Vallon, 1983
Translation copyright © Marion Boyars Publishers Ltd, 1991
Introduction copyright © Lila Azam Zanganeh, 2012
All rights reserved

The moral right of the author, translator and the author of the introduction has been asserted

Set in Monotype Dante
Typeset by Dinah Drazin
Printed in England by Clays Ltd, St Ives plc

ISBN: 978-0-141-19465-3

www.greenpenguin.co.uk

ALWAYS LEARNING   **PEARSON**

Contents

Contents

Introduction

To Mr Julian Green, in Paris

Dearest Mr Green,

Following a blitz investigation, I see that you were born in 1900, and that by the time you reached my age you were already an accomplished writer. However, I itch to tell you something straight off: we seem to share more than a few biographical details.

Like you, I was born in Paris to foreign parents. Like you, I chose to become a writer in a language that was not my own. Like you, I emigrated to New York. Like you, I feel an indescribable sort of happiness each time I set foot in this, our native city.

That said, I was stunned when I happened upon your *Paris* book for the first time. I'd started out reading your epigraph by Baudelaire: 'the shape of the city / Changes faster, alas, than the heart of mortal man ...' (from the 'Swan' in *Flowers of Evil*), and then skipped directly to the photo album, curious to see *your* ghostly Paris. And there ... what do I see? Photograph no. 6: 'A storm over the rue Vaneau, 1974 – taken from Julian Green's apartment window'. Though I wasn't yet born in 1974, I came of age on the rue Vaneau and, from my own balcony, at no. 72, on the sixth floor, I see exactly the same view as in your black-and-white photograph dating back nearly four decades! Presently, as I made my way through your book, I notice your description of the Montparnasse Tower, as seen from another window of your home. Now, there was another uncanny

coincidence. The house in which I grew up is angular and shaped in unusual ways. If I stand on the small mezzanine floor, facing the rue Vaneau, through a high window on the right, I too see the oblong black of the Montparnasse Tower! Yet, when you think back upon yourself as an eight-year-old boy bounding carefree down the streets of Paris, you write: 'Too much has changed for the worse in our city to let me smile at you as cheerfully as I should like.' But, say, Mr Green, perhaps the shape of our city has not changed so fast after all?

This would be very good news indeed. Because the Paris you describe in your book is nothing short of magical. Here is one of my favorite sentences: 'Paris is a city that might well be spoken of in the plural, as the Greeks used to speak of Athens, for there are many Parises, and the tourists' Paris is only superficially related to the Paris of the Parisians.' I like to think of the 's' in Paris as a poetic plural. With a twist, of course. You boldly go on defining the spell of this multiple Paris in terms of an ultra-specific type of urban boredom. 'Until you have wasted time in a city, you cannot pretend to know it well. The soul of a big city is not to be grasped so easily; in order to make contact with it, you have to have been bored, you have to have suffered a bit in those places that contain it. Anyone can get hold of a guide and tick off all the monuments, but within the very confines of Paris there is another city as difficult of access as Timbuktu once was.' According to you, those truly in the know never whisper a word about it, so that it's almost impossible for the outsider to seize upon the geography of this secret Paris. Except through the eyes of novelists and poets, whose role it is to see for the first time, as though with new eyes, the things others barely seem to notice. And this, precisely, is what your book affords us.

In fact, I can tell you that, after I read your book for the first time, I tried using it as a fanciful Baedeker. First, I examined a map of the city and, with a sudden smile, recalled your comment: 'I made the discovery that Paris was shaped like a human brain.' I also remembered that, during the war years, when you left for

the United States, you kept wondering how such a large city could fit so miraculously in a tiny compartment of the brain. Yet those bright, invisible neurons brought you all the bliss you needed: 'It was a Paris of visions in which I took my walks now, a Paris that, though intensely real, was imperceptibly migrating from flesh to spirit.' When you did return, you realized that the memories which had sustained you were so heartrendingly close to the concrete fabric of the city.

Content though you were at finding the suspended stairways of Montmartre, the wooded seclusion of Auteuil, or the trellised Passy of your childhood untouched, you began to worry that things you had most cherished were about to disappear. Oftentimes you caught yourself dreaming sadly of a Paris which, you suspected, no longer existed. But you also secretly thought that, the more vulnerable Paris appeared, the lovelier it was. How long would those seventeenth- and eighteenth-century houses still stand for? What would be left of them in ten or twenty years' time? What you perceived as frailty, or simply mortality, all at once alarmed and delighted you. You saw sadness reflected in sunshine; you felt the living crossing threads with the dead; you heard transient songs in times starved for poetry.

But may I be forthright with you, Mr Green? I don't much take to the nostalgic in you. Here is why: more than a century after your birth, I can tell you that Paris is just as exhilaratingly beautiful as it was when you were born. And I wonder if, like that painter in Proust's novel, *In Search of Lost Time*, artists are not meant to see that creatures of the future can be things of beauty in their own right ...

No, what I most love is when you talk about a Paris where time stops. One of your favourite places in the city happens to be mine, too. The Palais-Royal, behind the Louvre, with its seventeenth-century colonnade and aerial park. You see it as an enchanted forest, a maze where the lucky traveller cannot foresee where he'll wind up when he retraces his steps, a place where, once again,

graces are bestowed only upon those who know how to *waste time*. 'I felt I was on the threshold of a new country whose name figured in no book and where everything we think of as belonging to the material world was by some elusive mechanism becoming, as it were, the tangible aspect of the inner world.' There, you sense, the arrow of human time is reversed. 'I was advancing not so much in space as in memory, and not so much in the memory of my own life as in the scattered recollections of a whole race of men.'

Back on the city streets, however, you eye glimmers of beauty everywhere. In the contorted angel overlooking the rue Réaumur, the golden cap of the Val-de-Grâce gleaming at nighttime, the fast light shining on a Parisian face. You see the illusive texture of the secret courtyards and stairwells of Paris. Those 'circular stairwells, a residue of the dreams that they have sheltered, a memory, as it were, of the meditations in which love, lust, and world-weariness fought for the hearts of all the nameless people who ever passed that way'. Then, of course, there is the River Seine. Although, here, I am surprised you don't mention my favourite place in the entire city, Le Pré du Vert Galant, a tiny islet jutting off the pont Neuf. There is a weeping willow under which many a Parisian lover has lain for an idle hour. And any of us might have heard her speak just in the way you imagine: 'I have my moments of happiness in the June dawn … My memory is a great kaleidoscope in which you will find all that has gone to make up the history of your century.'

Unfortunately, Mr Green, I believe you died in 1998, so you might have just missed it, but the director Woody Allen made a film called *Everyone Says I Love You*, which I suspect you might have liked a lot. It takes place in New York, Venice and Paris. And Mr Allen seems in love with Paris very much in the same way you are. He, too, has his own moments of Paris. His bridges, his secret garrets, stairways and courtyards. The last scene is filmed late at night, near a bridge on the Ile Saint Louis. Allen's character waltzes with his ex-wife in a dream-like setting, as boats shine their lights on the emerald-green water. He lifts her up, and she glides in mid-air before falling

back into his arms. And I have often thought that this is exactly the city which, now and then, we Parisians catch a glimpse of at night, when we stay up late and decide to fall in love. It's the rush of our present, the 'rush of wonder'.

Yet you also imagine a man a thousand years from now, behind a windowpane, looking at a landscape of houses behind trees. You try to imagine having crossed that great length of time and being that man. 'What is he thinking about? Is he happy? … What does he believe? What can he see? This same curiosity that he arouses in me, others had about us before they passed away in the days when Lutetia was first emerging from the mud… And here am I, dreaming of that Paris of the future, raised up on the space that is now ours, where shuttered concrete, glass, steel, and possibly other materials as yet unknown will be the ingredients of a limitless beauty.' I love this inventory of your future, of your faith in us. This sudden certitude that beyond all her nights, Paris is still awake and alive.

Lila Azam Zanganeh, Paris, Summer 2011

PARIS

'... the shape of the city
Changes faster, alas, than the heart of mortal man ...'
Baudelaire, *The Flowers of Evil*
(LXXXIX, 'The Swan')

'... La Forme d'une ville
Change plus vite, hélas! que le coeur d'un mortel ...'
Baudelaire, *Les Fleurs du mal*
(LXXXIX, 'Le Cygne')

J'ai bien des fois rêvé d'écrire ...

J'ai bien des fois rêvé d'écrire sur Paris un livre qui fût comme une grande promenade sans but où l'on ne trouve rien de ce qu'on cherche, mais bien des choses qu'on ne cherchait pas. C'est même la seule façon dont je me sente capable d'aborder un sujet qui me décourage autant qu'il m'attire. Et tout d'abord, il me semble que je ne dirai mot des grands monuments et de tous les endroits où l'on s'attendrait à une description en règle. Pour les avoir trop regardées peut-être, je ne vois plus les gloires architecturales de Paris avec toute la liberté d'esprit nécessaire. Prévenu contre ou pour chacune d'elles, j'ai pris parti, je suis injuste. J'ai mille fois souhaité la tour Eiffel au fond de l'eau, il me plairait d'apprendre que les deux Palais, grand et petit, qui déshonorent le Cours-la-Reine ont disparu dans la nuit. Mes préférences vont aux vieilles pierres, je ne le cache pas, mais je pleurerais d'ennui s'il me fallait écrire une page sur l'hôtel des Invalides, parce que l'aimant comme je fais, je ne saurais vraiment qu'en dire. De même, je resterais muet devant Notre-Dame, retenu de parler, sans doute, par la honte de ce que je m'entendrais dire, et j'admire sans l'envier le courage de ceux que leur suffisance ou leur génie lance à l'assaut d'un tel monstre; pour ma part, j'aime mieux me taire, et Notre-Dame demeure pour moi Notre-Dame, un point, c'est tout.

A mes yeux Paris restera le décor d'un roman que personne n'écrira jamais. Que de fois je suis revenu de longues flâneries à travers de vieilles rues, le cœur lourd de tout ce que j'avais vu d'inexprimable! S'agit-il là d'une illusion? Je ne le crois pas. Il m'arrive

I have often dreamed of writing…

I have often dreamed of writing a book about Paris that would be
like one of those long, aimless strolls on which you find none of the
things you are looking for but many that you were not looking for.
In fact, that is the only way in which I feel I can tackle a subject that
I find as daunting as it is enticing. And let me say right away that
I shall be making no mention of the great monuments or any of
the places you would expect to find duly described. Possibly from
having looked at them too much, I can no longer see the architectural
glories of Paris with quite the open mind required. Tipped in favour
of or against each and every one of them in advance, my mind is
made up; I am not a fair judge. I have many times wished the Eiffel
Tower at the bottom of the ocean, and I should be delighted, to
learn that the two palaces, Great and Small, that disgrace the Cours-
la-Reine had disappeared during the night. I make no secret of the
fact that it is the old buildings I prefer, and yet I should be bored to
tears if I had to write a page about the Hôtel des Invalides. Loving
it as I do, I should really not know what to say. I should be similarly
struck dumb by Notre-Dame, my lips no doubt sealed by a sense of
shame at what I should hear them utter, and I admire (but do not
envy) the courage of those whose self-importance or sheer genius
prompts them to take on such a giant. I prefer to remain silent; for
me, Notre-Dame is simply Notre-Dame, full stop.

I shall always see Paris as the setting of a novel that will never
be written. The times I have returned from long walks through
ancient streets with my heart laden with all the inexpressible things

souvent de m'arrêter tout à coup devant telle grande croisée drapée de fausses dentelles, au fond d'un vieux quartier, et de rêver sans fin aux destinées inconnues qui se déroulent à l'abri de ces vitres noires. Mon regard distingue un petit bouquet qui change ou disparaît selon les saisons, placé au milieu d'une table que recouvre une étoffe sombre; et c'est tout, mais c'est peut-être assez. Qui vit, qui meurt entre ces murs? Pour un romancier, toute existence, fût-elle la plus simple, garde son irritant mystère, et la somme de tous les secrets que contient une ville a quelque chose qui tantôt le stimule et tantôt l'accable. Quel énorme gaspillage de situations, de mots, de coups de théâtre, de personnages, de mises en scène! Comment ne pas s'émouvoir d'une telle concurrence? Copier n'est pas possible. Il n'y a que les impuissants et les nigauds qui copient. Non, il s'agit de faire aussi bien, si l'on peut, avec des moyens à nous. Commence alors l'étrange supplice de la page blanche dans laquelle il faut ouvrir une fenêtre qui ne soit pas celle que j'ai vue tout à l'heure, mais d'une vérité aussi impérieuse.

Pendant les longues années de guerre que j'ai vécu loin de Paris, je me suis bien des fois demandé comment dans une petite case du cerveau humain pouvait tenir une aussi grande ville. Paris était devenu pour moi une sorte de monde intérieur dans lequel j'errais aux heures difficiles de l'aube, quand rôde le désespoir autour du dormeur qui s'éveille; mais il me fallut du temps pour franchir délibérément le seuil de cette ville secrète que je portais en moi, car il y eut d'abord les noires semaines durant lesquelles le seul nom de Paris broyait le cœur à qui l'entendait. Je me fermais donc à moi-même les portes de ma ville, j'en coupais les avenues du plus loin que cela m'était possible. La nuit, cependant, désobéissant à ma propre consigne, pareil à un espion ou à un voleur, je me glissais le long des rues, j'allais sans fin d'une maison à l'autre. J'apparaissais tout à coup dans une pièce où des amis se cachaient. 'Comment! C'est vous! C'est toi!' L'interminable dialogue s'ébauchait alors qui durait jusqu'au jour. Ce que nous ne pouvions nous dire, d'un rivage de l'Atlantique à l'autre, nous nous le disions cœur à cœur

I have seen! Is this an illusion? I think not. It happens frequently that, brought up short before, say, a large window draped with mock lace curtains, tucked away in one of the old quarters, I embark on an interminable fancy about the unknown destinies unfolding beyond its dark panes. My eye makes out a little bunch of flowers, which will change or disappear with the seasons, set in the middle of a table covered with a dark cloth; that is all, yet it may be enough. Who lives in that room? Who is dying between those four walls? In the novelist's eyes every life, even the humblest, possesses that itch of mystery, and there is something about the sum total of all the secrets contained in a city that he finds by turns stimulating and oppressive. What a prodigal waste of situations, speeches, dramas, characters, settings! Who would not be moved by such a struggle? Copying is out of the question; only fools and impotents copy. No, the thing is to produce something as good, if possible, out of your own resources. And so begins the strange torture of the blank sheet of paper, where you must open a window that is not the one I spotted just now but one equally insistent in its truthfulness.

During the long war years, when I was living far from Paris, I often used to wonder how so large a city found room inside a tiny compartment of the human brain. Paris, for me, had become a kind of inner world through which I roamed in those difficult dawn hours when despair lies in wait for the waking sleeper. I needed time, though, to take a conscious step over the threshold of this secret city that I was carrying round inside me; first there were the black weeks during which the mere mention of the name of Paris broke the hearts of all who heard it. So I barred the gates of my city against myself; I banished its avenues as far away as possible. At night, however, flouting my own orders, I would slink along its streets like a spy or a thief, restlessly going from house to house. Suddenly I would appear in a room where friends were hiding. 'What – *you* here? It *is* you!' And one of those interminable conversations would start up and not stop until daybreak. Things we could not tell one another with the width of the Atlantic between

dans ces entretiens hallucinés. Il n'y avait plus toute cette eau entre nous, j'avais aboli l'espace, j'étais là. Sans fin je voulais savoir. En sortant, je touchais de la main les pierres des maisons et le tronc des arbres, et je me retrouvais au réveil avec le bizarre sentiment d'avoir été à la fois comblé et frustré.

A force de songer à la capitale, je la reconstruisais en moi, et je remplaçais sa présence physique par autre chose de presque surnaturel à quoi je ne sais quel nom donner. Un plan de Paris fixé au mur retenait longuement mes regards et m'instruisait presque à mon insu. Je découvris que Paris avait la forme d'un cerveau humain.

Le souvenir me revint d'une tête d'homme fendue en deux que je regardais, enfant, à la devanture d'un opticien et qui faisait voir aux personnes curieuses tout l'intérieur de notre crâne. Avec un intérêt mêlé d'horreur, j'examinais cette masse blanche, rose et rouge, qui me donnait le cauchemar la nuit suivante. En vain, je me disais qu'il n'y avait là qu'un objet de carton ou de porcelaine, c'était malgré tout révoltant. Pour être juste, il fallait reconnaître chez les phrénologues le désir de ménager les natures sensibles comme la mienne en donnant à l'homme au crâne ouvert une expression d'indifférence aimable et presque amusée; cela ne lui faisait rien du tout d'avoir le cerveau à l'air et même il souffrait de bonne grâce qu'on lui eût collé de minuscules étiquettes sur chacune des circonvolutions, car c'était là l'intérêt de cette découverte: on avait peur, mais on devenait savant; on voyait, par exemple, où loge la mémoire, où l'invention, où les langues, où le raisonnement. Cela faisait horreur, mais on s'exaltait malgré tout à l'idée d'avoir sous les cheveux ce kilo de cervelle pensante et capable de tant de choses. Pour ma part, je me sentais à la fois fier et un peu malade. Aujourd'hui, l'homme des phrénologues ne ferait pas courir le plus léger frisson sur ma nuque, mais je n'ai pas fini de m'émerveiller de tout ce que notre cerveau peut accomplir avec un peu d'application; il n'est, au reste, que d'ouvrir un journal et de voir ce que nous avons fait du monde pour reconnaître en toute

us we communicated from heart to heart in those imaginary conversations. Gone was all the water that separated us; I had abolished space; I was there. I wanted to know everything. As I left I used to touch the stones of the houses and the trunks of the trees with my hand, and I would wake with a curious feeling of having been both fulfilled and frustrated.

Thinking about the capital all the time, I rebuilt it inside myself. I replaced its physical presence with something else, something almost supernatural; I don't know what to call it. A map of Paris pinned to the wall would hold my gaze for long periods, teaching me things almost subliminally. I made the discovery that Paris was shaped like a human brain.

A memory came back to me of a man's head split in two that I used to look at as a child in an optician's window and that displayed to the interested passer-by the entire contents of the human skull. I used to examine that mass of white, pink, and red with mingled curiosity and horror. It would give me nightmares the following night. No use my telling myself the thing was only made of cardboard or porcelain: it was revolting just the same. To be fair, the phrenologists had clearly wished to spare such sensitive natures as my own and had given the man with the cloven skull an expression of amiable, almost amused indifference. He had not the least objection to having his brain exposed, even taking it with a good grace that a tiny label had been glued to each convolution. Because that was the interesting thing about this discovery: you were scared, but you acquired knowledge; you saw, for example, where the memory was located, or the imagination, or languages, or the reasoning faculty. It was horrid, but even so you were excited by the idea that beneath your scalp there was this kilo of thinking grey matter that was capable of doing so much. I personally felt both proud and at the same time slightly sick. Nowadays the phrenologists' man would not send the least shiver down my spine, but I never cease to marvel at all our brains are able to accomplish with a little application. Why, you have only to open a newspaper and see what we have made of the world

9

impartialité que nous sommes des êtres vraiment supérieurs!

Quoi qu'il en soit, le plan de Paris m'aida plus d'un jour à passer des heures difficiles, et lui ayant trouvé la ressemblance que j'ai dite avec le cerveau humain, je m'efforçais de mettre dans les limites de cette ville toutes les circonvolutions observées jadis. Ainsi je me plaisais à croire que j'étais né dans le domaine de l'imagination et que j'avais grandi au milieu du souvenir; j'hésitais sur l'emplacement de la volonté, de la réflexion et du goût, je leur faisais sans cesse changer de quartier; parfois il me semblait naturel que la capitale se remémorât son histoire par le secours du Marais, qu'elle fît ses opérations intellectuelles avec l'aide du Ve arrondissement et ses calculs arithmétiques dans le quartier de la Bourse; mais traversant tout cela il y avait la Seine qui représentait à mes yeux ce que nous portons en nous d'instinctif et d'inexprimé, comme un grand courant d'inspirations incertaines qui cherche aveuglément une mer où se perdre …

Je ne prenais pas garde qu'avec le temps, ce Paris transposé risquait de devenir un peu plus abstrait chaque jour. Sans doute, je le voyais, je le regardais sans cesse, mais parfois le soupçon confus me venait que les pierres de ma ville se faisaient plus légères, comme si elles s'étaient mystérieusement vidées, et que je perdais tant soit peu le sentiment de leur dureté. Que ces choses sont difficiles à dire! C'était un Paris de visions dans lequel je me promenais maintenant, un Paris d'une réalité intense, mais qui émigrait imperceptiblement de la chair à l'esprit.

Dès les premières heures de mon retour en France, il me fut donné de comprendre à quel point la matière est parfois près de l'invisible où nous nous mouvons. Un désir ancien, presque un désir d'enfant me revint, un jour, de monter au sommet de Paris pour le voir le plus généralement possible. Que de fois, en Amérique, me reprochai-je de n'être jamais allé dans le dôme du Sacré-Cœur. Ce fut là que me conduisit une curiosité de provincial honteux à quoi se mêlaient les élans d'une vieille tendresse. Je fis donc l'ascension homicide, j'arrivai dans le ciel, je fermai les yeux dans un grand

to acknowledge quite impartially that we are truly superior beings!

Be that as it may, the map of Paris helped me on more than one occasion to get through some trying hours. Having hit upon this resemblance to the human brain, I sought to accommodate all the convolutions I had observed as a child within the confines of the city. For instance, it tickled my fancy to suppose I had been born in the realm of the imagination and had grown up in the domain of memory; unsure where to situate will, reflection, and judgement, I kept moving them from one district to another; sometimes it seemed right to me that the capital should recall its history through the medium of the Marais, perform its intellectual tasks with the aid of the fifth district, and do its sums in the Stock Exchange quarter; running through it all, however, there was the River Seine, which to my mind represented the instinctive, unspoken part of our nature, like a great current of vague inspirations blindly seeking an ocean in which to drown themselves …

I failed to notice that, as time went on, this transposed Paris was in danger of becoming a little more abstract each day. I could see it all right, I used to look at it all the time, but I would occasionally be visited by a dim suspicion that the stones of my city were somehow shedding weight, as if they had mysteriously been emptied of their substance, and that I was gradually losing all sense of their hardness. How difficult it is to say these things! It was a Paris of visions in which I took my walks now, a Paris that, though intensely real, was imperceptibly migrating from flesh to spirit.

Within hours of my return to France I had occasion to appreciate how close matter sometimes comes to the invisible sphere in which we move. One day an old urge, almost a childhood urge, came back to me: to climb to the highest point in Paris in order to gain as wide a view of it as possible. How often had I reproached myself, in America, with never having been up to the dome of Sacré Coeur, the Church of the Sacred Heart! That was where I was now driven by the curiosity of the apologetic visitor from the sticks mixed with the promptings of a former love. So I made the

chavirement d'entrailles, puis rouvrant de force mes paupières, je regardai. Il me sembla que je recevais la ville tout entière dans la poitrine. Ce fut ainsi qu'elle me fut rendue. L'hiver finissait; déjà l'aveuglante lumière de mars dévorait tout, et à perte de vue Paris était là, portant comme un manteau qui lui glissait à tout moment des épaules l'ombre des grands nuages que le vent chassait d'un coin à l'autre du ciel.

Cette énorme masse de pierre, je l'avais vue trop de fois pour en être surpris. Pourtant, comme elle gardait bien son mystère et avec quelle sombre violence elle existait! Noire, semée de petites taches de soleil qui imitaient le scintillement des vagues à la surface d'une mer inquiète, elle n'était pas belle, elle était immense, elle excédait tous les efforts qu'eût fourni l'imagination pour se représenter les royaumes du monde assemblés à nos pieds, et dans sa démesure, il y avait un excès qui provoquait l'inquiétude comme un défi à des lois non écrites, mais redoutables.

Elle était manifestement la ville qui attire la colère, la ville sans cesse en danger parce que, devant les tentations de toutes les grandeurs possibles, elle n'a jamais su faire le grand refus qui l'eût mise à l'abri de son destin. Ses dômes et ses tours donnent d'une manière indéfinissable l'impression de tenir tête à quelqu'un, et dans la façon même dont ils sont posés sur cette plaine houleuse, il y a quelque chose d'opiniâtre, de superbe et d'insoumis. La ville, en effet, ne sourit qu'à ceux qui flânent dans ses rues; à ceux-là, elle parle un langage rassurant et familier, mais l'âme de Paris ne se révèle que de loin et de haut, et c'est dans le silence du ciel que s'entend le grand cri pathétique d'orgueil et de foi qu'elle élève vers les nuages.

murderous climb, reached the sky, shut my eyes against the churning of my stomach, then prised my eyelids open and looked. It was as if the whole city hit me in the chest. That was how I got it back. Winter was drawing to a close; the dazzling March light already consumed everything, and as far as the eye could see there was Paris, wearing, like a cloak that kept slipping from its shoulders, the shadow of the great clouds that the wind was chasing across the breadth of the sky.

I had seen that vast mass of stone too many times for it to surprise me. Yet how well it preserved its mystery! The brooding violence of its existence! Black, flecked with sunlight in a way that mimicked the sparkling of waves on the surface of a restless sea, it was not beautiful, it was immense, surpassing every effort the imagination might have made to picture the kingdoms of the world assembled at our feet, and in its disproportion there was a quality of excess that aroused anxiety, as if a challenge had been hurled at some formidable, unwritten law.

It was manifestly the city that attracts anger, the city that is in constant danger because, tempted by every possible form of greatness, it has never been able to utter the big no that would have saved it from its fate. In some indefinable way its domes and towers give the impression of standing up to someone; the very manner of their distribution over the heaving plain gives them an obstinate, arrogant, insubordinate look. Certainly the city's smile is reserved for those who draw near and loaf in its streets; to them it speaks a familiar, reassuring language. The soul of Paris, however, can be apprehended only from afar and from above, and it is in the silence of the sky that you hear the great and moving cry of pride and faith it upraises to the clouds.

Passy

Rester assis sur les genoux du modèle qu'on se propose de peindre ne m'a jamais paru la position la plus favorable. Si peu de recul qu'on prenne, on y gagne. Aussi m'est-il difficile d'écrire une ligne sur Paris alors que je m'y trouve: il faut que je me lève et que je m'en aille. D'ici, de Copenhague, je le vois très bien. Des mouettes se laissent glisser devant ma fenêtre avec leur étrange petit cri d'enfant malade, et voilà que la brume se déchire autour des clochers vert amande.

De quoi Passy avait-il l'air? A bien y réfléchir, je ne sais plus très bien. J'y vais quelquefois, mais trop de souvenirs y viennent à ma rencontre qui le transforment à mes yeux. J'ai assez peu d'attaches au vieux quartier que j'habite maintenant à Paris, le septième, et quand je me promène dans Passy, il me semble que j'erre à l'intérieur de moi-même, et je bute sans cesse contre mon enfance.

La frontière était au bas de la rue Raynouard. Il y avait là deux pentes si raides qu'on pouvait raisonnablement espérer y voir s'emballer les chevaux de fiacre, ce qui arrivait quelquefois, soit qu'ils descendissent au grand galop la rue que je viens de nommer, soit qu'ils prissent le mors aux dents sur les flancs vertigineux de la rue de Boulainvilliers. En face du pavillon où nous étions logés se voyaient d'inquiétants gazomètres, posés au bord du ciel comme d'immenses tambours noirs. Plus loin, de l'autre côté de la place, c'était Auteuil et les platanes de la rue La Fontaine, mais nous n'allions pas souvent de ce côté-là; nous étions de Passy. En soufflant un peu, nous remontions vers les hauteurs. J'avançais, un petit-beurre au poing.

Passy

Sitting in the lap of the model you intend to paint has never seemed to me to be the ideal position. Step back even a pace and you gain by it. So I find it hard to write anything about Paris while I am there: I have to get up and go away. From here, in Copenhagen, I see it very clearly. Seagulls slide past my window, uttering their curious little cry, like a sick child's, and the almond-green bell-towers shred the drifting mist.

What used Passy to look like? Thinking about it, I can't really remember. I visit the place occasionally, but too many memories come out to meet me, changing the way I see it. I have few links with the old quarter in which I now live in Paris, the seventh district, and when I go walking in Passy I seem to be wandering around inside myself; I am constantly bumping into my childhood.

The border was at the bottom of the rue Raynouard. There were a couple of slopes there so steep that you could reasonably expect to see cab horses bolting, as they did occasionally, either hurtling down the aforementioned street at full gallop or being reined in hard on the dizzying gradient of the rue de Boulainvilliers. From the house where we lived you saw these disturbing gas holders, set down at the edge of the sky like great black drums. Farther off, on the other side of the square, was Auteuil and the plane trees of the rue La Fontaine. We didn't often go that way, though; we were Passyites. Puffing a bit, we would climb the hill, I with a biscuit clutched in one hand. To our right the old town houses stood shoulder to shoulder, checked in a corporate slide,

Sur la droite, les vieux hôtels s'épaulaient les uns les autres, arrêtés dans une glissade générale, et nous regardions, les joues prises entre les barreaux des grilles, des jardins merveilleux dont les lointains bleuâtres, comme dans un tableau, allaient rejoindre les rives de la Seine. Cela me paraissait aussi beau qu'un décor du Châtelet, mais mon ravissement était porté à son comble lorsqu'on nous permett-ait de descendre les marches qui menaient à la rue Berton. J'avais alors l'illusion de me trouver à la campagne. Comme tout Parisien né, je m'ennuie aux champs, ce qui n'empêche pas qu'à certains jours j'éprouve un violent désir de m'étendre sur de l'herbe et de respirer les bonnes odeurs de la terre, quitte au bout d'un petit quart d'heure à languir après mes rues et mes boutiques. Quoi qu'il en soit, à l'époque dont je parle, la rue Berton était encore une longue rue de village qui cheminait entre des murs couronnés d'arbres. On pouvait facilement s'y croire à une heure de Paris. Le silence y était profond et nos pas sur les grosses pierres rondes faisaient un bruit qui n'était pas le bruit qu'on entend dans les villes. Une lanterne se balançait au vent, je le jure, et il y avait une borne marquant la limite des seigneuries de Passy et d'Auteuil. Cela me grisait de pouvoir me dire que je vivais dans la seigneurie de Passy. La nostalgie d'autrefois était chez moi si forte que ces simples mots suffisaient à me jeter dans une tristesse délicieuse. Passé la maison de Balzac et le parc de l'hôtel de Lamballe, la rue tournait à angle droit et continuait jusqu'à la Seine, alors qu'aujourd'hui elle cesse tout à coup d'exister et le tronçon qui en reste ne donne qu'une faible idée de l'exquise venelle du XVIIIe siècle. Ce qu'est devenu ce coin de Passy me paraît d'une laideur si morne et si banale qu'elle provoque, me semble-t-il, moins l'indignation que l'ennui et le calme désespoir dont parle Emerson. Par une journée d'hiver un peu sombre, avec une bise coupante sous un ciel bas, je ne vois pas de meilleur décor pour un suicide ou pour une exécution capitale. On demeure stupéfait de ce qu'un quart de siècle a pu faire pour priver de son charme cette partie de la ville. Je sais qu'il est inutile et ridicule de se lamenter sur la disparition des vieilles pierres, mais c'est un regard dépourvu

and pressing our cheeks between the gate bars we used to gaze into marvellous gardens whose bluish distances, as in a painting, ran down to the banks of the Seine. To me that was as lovely as a stage set. My delight knew no bounds, however, when we were allowed to descend the steps leading to the rue Berton. I had the illusion, then, of being in the country. Like all native Parisians, I find the country boring, but that doesn't stop me experiencing a violent desire, some days, to be lying in the grass, inhaling the good odours of the earth – even if a mere quarter of an hour later I am pining for my streets and shops. Be that as it may, at the time I am talking about, the rue Berton was still a long village street running between tree-capped walls. You might easily have thought you were an hour's journey from Paris. Deep silence reigned, and the sound of our footsteps on the huge round stones was not like the sound you hear in towns. A streetlamp swung in the wind, I swear it did, and there was a stone marking where the manors of Passy and Auteuil met. It gave me a great thrill to be able to tell myself I lived in the manor of Passy. Nostalgia for another age was so strong in me that the mere words sufficed to plunge me into a delicious melancholy. Past Balzac's house and the grounds of Lamballe House the road turned at right angles and continued as far as the Seine, whereas today it comes to an abrupt halt, and the short stretch that is left gives only a faint idea of the exquisite eighteenth-century ride. What has happened to this corner of Passy strikes me as so dismal and trite in its ugliness as to provoke, I think, not so much indignation as boredom and Emerson's 'quiet despair'. On a dull winter's day, with a sharp North wind gusting under a lowering sky, I can think of no finer setting for a suicide or an execution. It is quite astonishing how a quarter of a century has contrived to strip this part of the city of its charm. I know it is pointless and absurd to mourn the passing of old bits of stone, but there is certainly no indulgence in the look I direct at the fortress-like blocks of flats that now tower above the high ground where I remember seeing rows of villas,

d'indulgence que je tourne vers les immeubles à profil de forteresse qui dominent les hauteurs où je me souviens avoir vu des rangées de villas d'une élégance surannée et des jardins conservant comme un trésor leur silence et leurs chants d'oiseaux.

L'autre Passy, le Passy prospère, m'était en horreur alors même que j'étais enfant. Il existait une forme de richesse qui me donnait envie de pleurer par ce qu'elle avait de sévère et d'arrogant, avec ces balcons pleins de morgue, ces portes cochères qui disaient non, et ces luxueuses loges de concierge. Mais ce Passy-là n'était pas le vrai. Je faisais une distinction entre le seizième et la seigneurie de Passy, le vieux village de Passy qui dévalait au sud de l'ancienne Grand-rue qui s'appela (horreur!) rue Marat avant de s'appeler rue de Passy. De ce petit univers auquel je dois tant, on ne retrouve aujourd'hui que de pauvres débris. Gautier affirmait que le Paris de sa jeunesse était devenu méconnaissable. Pour ma part, lorsque je descends des hauteurs de Passy vers la Seine, je me demande parfois où je suis, et si je n'ai pas rêvé. Seules me consolent du désastre les profondeurs de l'avenue Henri-Martin encore intacte, quand, au début de l'été, la voûte opaque des marronniers veille sur un reste de fraîcheur et que, dans ce verdoyant tunnel coupé de raies lumineuses, je vois un cavalier oublieux de son temps et qui fuit au galop vers Hier.

outmoded in their elegance, and gardens enshrining treasures of silence and birdsong.

The other Passy, the prosperous Passy, I loathed even as a child. There was a kind of wealth that made me want to weep because of a certain quality of severity and arrogance in those strutting balconies, unwelcoming carriage entrances, and sumptuous porter's lodges. But that was not the real Passy. I drew a distinction between the sixteenth district and the manor of Passy, the old village of Passy that tumbled down the hill to the south of the former high street, once named (ghastly thought!) after Marat before it became known as the rue de Passy. Of that world in miniature to which I owe so much, nothing is left nowadays but a few poor fragments. Gautier said that the Paris of his youth had become unrecognizable. When I walk down from Passy towards the Seine, I sometimes wonder where I am and whether I have not been dreaming. My sole consolation in disaster lies in the depths of the as yet intact avenue Henri-Martin when, in early summer, the impenetrable vault of the horse-chestnut trees protects a residue of coolness, and I spy, in this verdant tunnel lit by shafts of sunlight, a lone horseman, oblivious of his time, fleeing at full gallop in the direction of Yesterday.

Saint-Julien-le-Pauvre

C'est au milieu des flammes de l'été qu'il convient de pousser la porte un peu disjointe refermée sur des trésors de fraîcheur. J'entre et me tiens immobile. Ici la grande voix de Paris n'arrive plus qu'en un murmure que domine le plus grand silence de cette petite église. Les piliers trapus sont tout roses dans la lumière de l'après-midi qui tombe des fenêtres étroites au vitrage blanc serti de carreaux bleus. Ils soutiennent le berceau roman sous lequel vole la pensée comme un oiseau sous les branches d'un bois; ils sont si forts et si tranquilles qu'on dirait qu'ils attendent le jugement dernier dans une contemplation qui les sépare du siècle, et comme des rois absorbés par des rêves de grandeur ils dédaignent la triste inquiétude moderne dont j'ai ma part et me font, sans même le savoir, l'aumône d'un peu de cette paix qu'ils gardent en eux. Des couronnes de feuillages sont posées sur leur tête et ils les portent au-devant de l'autel ainsi que des corbeilles d'offrandes en une procession qui dure depuis huit siècles; là, une sirène ailée, ailleurs un chevalier chrétien sont comme les symboles des graves pensées qu'ils mènent sous le ciel arrondi des voûtes.

A cet endroit, peut-être, Dante s'est agenouillé entre ces murs verdis où l'on croirait qu'un océan a traîné ses algues; ici, le visionnaire a salué l'invisible et il s'est souvenu plus tard de la petite rue parisienne où sa méditation s'est un instant reposée dans son voyage vers les abîmes du monde intérieur.

Aujourd'hui, il est bien difficile d'imaginer le fastueux passé de Saint-Julien-le-Pauvre qui semble avoir attendu nos tristes temps

St Julian the Poor

A scorching hot summer's day is the right time to push open the slightly rickety door that shuts off a treasure trove of coolness. I enter and stand motionless. In here the great shout of Paris is reduced to a murmur, overpowered by the greater silence of this little church. The stocky pillars glow pink in the afternoon light that falls from narrow windows of clear glass set between panes of blue. The pillars support the Romanesque barrel vault, beneath which thought takes wing like a bird beneath a woodland canopy. They are so strong, so still, as if waiting for the Last Judgement, lost in a kind of contemplation that cuts them off from our century. Like kings engrossed in dreams of greatness, they scorn the sad modern anxiety of which I have my share and make me, unawares, a gift of some of the peace they hold within them. Crowns of foliage are set on their heads, and they bear them towards the altar like baskets of offerings in a procession that has been going on for eight hundred years; a winged siren here, a Christian knight there are like symbols of the solemn thoughts they harbour beneath the rounded sky of the vaults.

This could be the spot where Dante knelt, between these green-stained walls that look as if an ocean has draped them with its algae; this was where the visionary hailed the invisible, and he later recalled the narrow Paris street where his meditation had enjoyed a moment's respite on its journey towards the abysses of the inner world.

It is hard to imagine the sumptuous past of St Julian the Poor today. The church appears to have waited for our sad modern age

modernes pour mériter pleinement son vocable. Nous ne pouvons que faiblement entrevoir cette église à l'époque où un prieuré lui était adjoint et où cinquante religieux chantaient sous ses voûtes, et l'on a quelque peine à se rendre compte qu'une des plus belles cérémonies du Moyen Age se soit déroulée dans ce lieu que notre pauvreté spirituelle a rendu si humble. C'est là pourtant que le *rector magnificus* de la Sorbonne remettait à son successeur le manteau d'hermine et le sac de velours contenant le sceau de l'université. C'est là encore que, le 11 juin de chaque année, le corps universitaire s'assemblait en grande pompe pour se rendre ensuite à la foire du lendit où il achetait le parchemin dont il avait besoin. Dès l'aube, la rue Galande, la rue du Fouarre, la rue Saint-Séverin et la rue Saint-Jacques étaient réveillées par les tambours et les trompettes des écoliers dont beaucoup brandissaient des lances, des épées ou des bâtons sans autre raison que leur jeunesse et un goût naturel pour le tumulte. De toute cette vie pleine, forte et joyeuse qui fut la vie d'une époque que nous n'égalons pas, que reste-t-il dans ce quartier, hormis un nom? C'est celui de la rue du Fouarre qui me fait ressouvenir que le pape Urbain V enjoignit aux étudiants de s'asseoir non sur des bancs, mais bien aux pieds de leur maître; or, s'asseoir sur le sol est dur, et les garçons coururent chez les marchands de *feurre* ou de paille qui vendaient leur marchandise à l'ombre de Saint-Julien. Rien ne nous empêche de croire que Dante fit comme tout le monde et s'en fut chercher sa botte de paille à cet endroit pour aller écouter les leçons de son bon maître Brunetto Latini, qu'il précipita ensuite en enfer, quitte, par une manière de compensation, à glisser le nom de la petite rue du Fouarre dans un tercet du Paradis.

Le XVIIe siècle secoua sa perruque ignorante devant la vénérable église et la jugea barbare. Sans doute la crut-il trop insignifiante pour la moderniser tout à fait; sans doute aussi, Saint-Julien, à l'extrême limite du roman, mais déjà soumis aux premiers étirements du nouveau style, n'avait-il pas aux yeux des contemporains de Mansart ce caractère gothique qui leur chauffait la bile et qu'ils

in order fully to deserve its name. We catch only a feeble glimpse of the way it was when a priory adjoined it and fifty monks filled its vaults with the sound of their chanting, and it is difficult for us to appreciate that one of the loveliest ceremonies of the Middle Ages was held in a place that our spiritual poverty has brought so low. Yet this is where the *rector magnificus* of the Sorbonne handed over the ermine cloak and the velvet bag containing the seal of the university to the person who was to succeed him. It was here, too, that on June 11 each year the teaching staff gathered with great pomp before proceeding to the annual fair in St Denis Fields to purchase their parchment requirement. The rue Galande, the rue du Fouarre, the rue Saint-Séverin, and the rue Saint-Jacques would be roused at dawn by the drums and trumpets of the students, many of whom brandished spears, swords, or sticks for no other reason than that they were young and loved a rumpus. Of all that full, strong, joyous life that belonged to an age we cannot match, what is left in this quarter, apart from one name? It is that of the rue du Fouarre, which reminds me of when Pope Urban V enjoined students to sit not on benches but actually at the feet of their masters. The ground being hard to sit on, the lads would go running to the street vendors who sold straw for stuffing in the shadow of St Julian. There is nothing to stop us picturing Dante doing as everyone else did and coming here for his bundle of straw before attending the lessons of his excellent master Brunetto Latini, whom he subsequently pitched into hell, though he did in a way make up for it by slipping the name of the little rue du Fouarre into a tercet of the *Paradiso*.

The seventeenth century shook its ignorant wig at the venerable church and pronounced it barbaric. No doubt it was not thought significant enough for wholesale modernization; probably, too, St Julian, situated on the very edge of the Romanesque, though already subject to the first stretchings of the new style, did not strike Mansart's contemporaries as possessing the Gothic character that so got their goat and that they did their best to obliterate in

s'efforcèrent d'oblitérer dans le chœur de Saint-Séverin, voisin plus malheureux de Saint-Julien-le-Pauvre. Ce fut pourtant le prieur même de Saint-Julien qui raccourcit la nef et remplaça le portail roman par une façade que cet âne tonsuré croyait dorique. De nos jours, dernier avatar, une large iconostase installée par des popes venus d'Orient coupe en deux ce qui reste d'une des plus belles et des plus anciennes églises de Paris.

Telle qu'elle est, cependant, l'église a conservé sa grâce robuste et sa mystérieuse jeunesse. On l'imagine au milieu des prés, car elle a le charme d'une église de campagne. Sa face solide et naïve est loin des élans fiévreux de Saint-Séverin qui se replie sur lui-même et se pare de grands lambeaux d'ombre. Saint-Julien accueille le jour et retient jusqu'au crépuscule la lumière entre ses murs; il est carré, ferme et placide comme un raisonnement de saint Thomas. Ni le doute ni les visions chagrines ne viendront jamais troubler sa solitude pensive et sereine. C'est un religieux au cœur simple, assis dans sa robe blanche sur les bords du fleuve gaulois.

Naguère, lorsqu'on poussait la petite porte latérale à l'intérieur de l'église, on se trouvait dans un charmant terrain vague où le pied heurtait dans l'herbe haute des pierres qui étaient parmi les plus vieilles de Paris. Tout près du chevet de Saint-Julien, un des derniers vestiges du mur dit de Philippe Auguste saillait tout à coup des graminées comme un rocher sort de la mer, et un arbre tordu mourait lentement sous le poids de plusieurs siècles, poussant encore des feuilles qui palpitaient dans le ciel. Qui se souvient de ce lieu si bien accordé à la rêverie? Au loin, les tours de Notre-Dame qui se font blanches dans l'orage, paraissaient noires contre le ciel de juillet, et de temps à autre, un remorqueur sur la Seine jetait un long appel mélancolique dont la note brumeuse traînait et s'effaçait au fond de l'azur. Mais la rumeur de Paris semblait mourir aux limites de cette petite solitude où j'aimais à réfléchir. Le silence autour de moi était comme une demeure où le passé avait pris refuge; il me semblait que toute une France romane habitait cette paix intérieure dont les vieilles pierres de Saint-Julien présentaient

the choir of St Séverin, St Julian's less fortunate neighbour. But it was the prior of St Julian himself who shortened the nave and replaced the Romanesque portico with a façade that that tonsured ass believed to be Doric. Latterly, in a final metamorphosis, a wide iconostasis put in by Eastern Orthodox priests bisects what is left of one of the loveliest and most ancient churches in Paris.

Even so, St Julian the Poor has kept its sturdy grace and mysterious youthfulness. You can imagine it surrounded by fields, for it has the charm of a country church. Its solid, artless countenance is so different from the fevered flights of St Séverin, which withdraws into itself behind great tatters of shadow. St Julian embraces the day and holds the light in its walls until dusk; it is as four-square, firm, and placid as a Scholastic argument. Neither doubt nor distressing visions will ever disturb its pensive, serene solitude. It is a simple-hearted divine, sitting in his white robe on the bank of the Gallic river.

You used to be able to push open the little side door inside the church and find yourself in a delightful piece of waste ground, covered with vegetation, where your feet might stumble against some of the oldest stones in Paris. Hard by the chevet of St Julian one of the last vestiges of 'Philippe Auguste's Wall' stuck up abruptly out of the long grass like a rock emerging from the sea, and a twisted tree, slowly dying beneath the weight of several centuries, still sprouted leaves that quivered overhead. Who remembers that place, so attuned to day-dreaming? In the distance the towers of Notre-Dame, white in stormy weather, looked black against the July sky, and the occasional tugboat on the Seine would utter a long-drawn-out, melancholy cry, the misty note lingering and fading into the blue beyond. Yet the hubbub of Paris seemed to die at the edges of that small solitude where I loved to come and think. The silence around me was like a dwelling in which the past had sought refuge; that inner peace seemed to me to hold a real feeling of Romanesque France, of which St Julian's ancient stones offered a tangible image. That was what so attracted me in

une image sensible. C'était cela qui m'attirait, aux environs de ma seizième année. J'avais découvert la petite église au hasard d'une promenade, j'y revins bien des fois depuis.

Il arrive que nous fassions sans le savoir des gestes dont le sens ne nous apparaît que beaucoup plus tard et qui semblent pourtant avoir été dictés par la partie la plus vigilante de nous-mêmes. Au printemps de 40, qui se termina si tragiquement pour l'Europe civilisée, je me rendis d'instinct vers les endroits de Paris où j'avais le plus de souvenirs et certaines églises me retinrent longtemps, dont je ne pensais pas être privé de si tôt. Saint-Julien fut celle que je trouvai le plus difficile à quitter: le seuil passé pour sortir, je le repassai un moment plus tard, pris d'une inquiétude trop vague pour que les mots pussent la traduire, et je promenai un dernier regard sur ces piliers où le soleil couchant posait un reflet mélancolique.

my sixteenth year or thereabouts. Having come across the little church by accident on one of my walks, I went back there again and again.

Sometimes we do things, without thinking, that make no sense to us until much later and yet appear to have been prompted by the most alert part of our being. In the spring of 1940, which ended so tragically for civilized Europe, I instinctively visited those places in Paris where I had most memories, and certain churches detained me at length, though I did not then imagine I should be deprived of them so soon. St Julian was the one I found hardest to leave: having crossed the threshold on my way out, I re-crossed it a moment later, touched by a misgiving too vague to find expression in words, and took one last look at those columns, which the setting sun had invested with a melancholy glow.

Les hauteurs du seizième

C'est à peu près vers ces moments de l'année, au début d'avril, que les marronniers du Trocadéro se mettent à reverdir. Il y en a un, entre autres, qui étend ses branches au-dessus d'une grille du Métropolitain et prospère innocemment dans de tièdes et méphitiques effluves. Ses feuilles naissantes s'ouvrent, puis s'écarquillent comme de petites mains avides. Dans peu de temps il aura ses chandelles, et si j'ai bon souvenir elles seront rouges. Il est jeune; c'est un petit Parisien précoce et farceur qui trouve que sa ville sent bon et qui arrive le premier au seuil du printemps, avec tout son feuillage et tous ses lampions. Du temps que nous habitions, lui et moi, la même ville, je l'appelais le marronnier du métro et j'avais pour lui cette amitié particulière qu'on ne donne qu'aux arbres.

Depuis que, par un phénomène singulier, le Trocadéro s'est envolé en ne nous laissant que ses ailes, la place a beaucoup changé. Quelques années auparavant, elle donna un grand coup d'épaule dans la direction du cimetière qui perdit le charmant escalier par où l'on montait à la rue des Réservoirs; les marches n'étaient pas bien hautes; en levant les yeux, on apercevait une rangée de cyprès noirs qui parlaient de l'au-delà en termes convenus et séparaient des vivants les ombres de Marie Bashkirtseff et d'Edouard Manet. En bas, le bonhomme Franklin regardait d'un œil satisfait passer les autobus, après avoir jeté en tas ses in-folio de bronze sous son fauteuil. Il y avait dans tout cela une sorte d'incohérence qui finissait par plaire.

La rue Franklin est une boiteuse qui descend en clopinant vers la rue de Passy. A la hauteur du cimetière, ses maisons jettent la vue

The superior sixteenth district

It is around this time of year, in early April, that the Trocadero chestnut trees start to turn green. There is one that stretches out its branches over a metro grating and takes innocent advantage of the warm, noxious exhalations. Its new leaves open up, then spread wide like greedy little hands. Before long it will have its candles, and, if I remember rightly, they will be red. The tree is a young one, a precocious, mischievous Parisian stripling who finds that his city smells good and who is the first to reach the threshold of spring with all his foliage and all his paper lanterns. In the days when we shared the same city, he and I, I called him the 'metro chestnut' and felt that special friendship towards him that we grant only to trees.

Since the Trocadero Palace flew away by some strange phenomenon, leaving only its wings, the open space in front of it has changed a great deal. Some years ago it gave a great lurch towards the cemetery, which lost the charming flight of steps that used to lead up to the rue des Réservoirs. The steps were not particularly steep. Looking up, you saw a row of black cypresses that spoke of the beyond in conventional terms and stood between the living and the shades of Marie Bashkirtseff and Edouard Manet. Lower down, old man Franklin cast a contented eye on the passing buses, having thrown his bronze folios in a heap under his chair. There was a sort of incoherence about it all that was ultimately pleasing.

The rue Franklin is a crippled old lady hobbling down to meet the rue de Passy. Level with the cemetery, her houses look out over

par-dessus une aile du Trocadéro et l'on dirait qu'elles se haussent sur la pointe des pieds pour découvrir la partie perdue entre le Panthéon et les Invalides. Son regard plonge un moment dans les profondeurs de cave des jardins et des allées où l'ombre rôde en plein midi, puis elle lance au bout de la rue Le Tasse un bref coup d'œil vers la tour Eiffel pour voir si elle est toujours là, et brusquement elle descend plus vite, entre les débits de tabac et les marchands de bric-à-brac, jusqu'au carrefour Delessert que surveille un neurasthénique bec de gaz, à l'entrée de la rue de Passy.

Rue de Passy, je sais par cœur tes boutiques, tes marchands de bas sous les portes cochères, tes panonceaux dédorés et les peintures sur marbre de tes crèmeries, et les ciels de tes pâtisseries, Coquelin, Petit et Bourbonneux, et le marchand d'huîtres au milieu de ses paniers avec son petit couteau, et le marchand de chaussures où ma bonne Lina achetait ses pantoufles à pompons azur, et la papeterie où les mouches se chauffent au soleil, sur les couvertures des livres de classe, et l'austère magasin de Nicolas, le marchand de vins, et la pharmacie de Monsieur Beaudichon qui avait une si belle barbe, et les grosses lettres d'or qui révèlent à tout le monde, des hauteurs d'un balcon vertigineux, la présence du chirurgien-dentiste, et la tête de cheval, dorée aussi, au-dessus de la porte du manège, et l'horlogerie où le patron, coupé en deux sur son établi, répare une petite montre, et les célestes effluves des premières branches de lilas que la fleuriste aux doigts rouges abrite sous la voûte du 93, et les moutons écorchés, chastement ceints de tabliers blancs, parmi les guirlandes de laurier de la boucherie, dans le gonflement solennel des rideaux rayés de vermillon, et la charmante camelote du parfumeur, et les bocaux de l'herboriste, et les regards que les mitrons lancent vers les mollets des ménagères, dans les soupiraux des boulangeries, et les batailles de chiens, et les collisions de paniers dont les pans se heurtent comme des poupes de galères hostiles, et les cris, les rires, le fracas des bus qui roulent à fond sur tout ce monde et n'écrasent pas le bout d'un seul orteil, et la belle natte liquide que tresse le ruisseau le long du trottoir...

one wing of the Trocadero, apparently standing on tiptoe for a sight of the match – a foregone conclusion – between the Pantheon and the Invalides. Her gaze plunges for a moment into the cavernous depths of gardens and driveways where shadows still lurk at noon. Then, at the end of the rue Le Tasse, she casts a quick glance in the direction of the Eiffel Tower to check that it is still there before scurrying on down between the tobacconists and the junkshops to the crossroads at the bottom, with its dejected gaslamp standing sentinel at the entrance to the rue de Passy.

Ah, rue de Passy – I know your shops by heart, your stocking sellers in the wide doorways, your once-gilded signs, the paintings on marble in your dairies, and the heavens of your confectioners, Coquelin, Petit, and Bourbonneux, and the oyster-seller with his baskets all around him and his little knife, and the shoeshop where Lina, my nanny, used to buy those slippers with the sky-blue pom-poms, and the stationer's where flies basked in the sun on the covers of the exercise books, and the grim Nicolas shop, the wine merchant's, and Mr Beaudichon's pharmacy (he had such a beautiful beard), and the great gold letters high up on a balcony, proclaiming to all and sundry that a dental surgeon lived here, and the horse's head, likewise gilded, above the gate of the riding school, and the clockmaker's where the proprietor, cut in two by his workbench, sat repairing a tiny watch, and the heavenly fragrance of the first sprays of lilac that the florist with the red hands kept in the shade beneath the archway of number 93, and the flayed sheep in their chaste white aprons, hanging up amid garlands of bay in the butcher's shop, surrounded by solemn bulges of scarlet-striped curtains, and the perfumer's charming trumpery, and the herbalist's bowls, and the glances the assistants would dart at the housewives' legs from the basement windows of the bakeries, and the dog fights, and the baskets colliding like the prows of warring galleys, and the shouts, the laughter, the roar of the buses that would drive full tilt into all those people and never so much as run over the tip of a single toe, and the lovely plait of liquid that the gutter drew along the kerb...

Dans les insomnies du petit jour, il m'arrive de refaire cette promenade impossible, et si la fantaisie me prend d'aller, comme autrefois, porter des livres à mon relieur, qui n'habite pas loin de la rue Raynouard, j'hésite entre la rue de l'Annonciation et la rue Jean-Bologne, et presque toujours je choisis cette dernière à cause de son chantier à charbon dont la beauté inhumaine a le charme horrifiant d'un paysage lunaire. Je veux regarder les pyramides noires au fond éclaboussé d'argent, et les stères de bûches à l'architecture babylonienne; il m'est agréable de respirer là l'odeur immémoriale du bois, de l'anthracite et du coke, et quittant l'entrepôt où j'ai promené des rêves de somnambule, de me retrouver dans la petite rue que termine une église de village.

Suivons-la, cette rue où nous croiserons les fantômes de nos premières années. Cours, écolier, avec ton cartable qui saute à chaque pas entre tes épaules, crie, crie pour rien, pour le plaisir d'être sur terre, jette en passant un regard à la boutique de l'antiquaire où le chat gris dort entre les yatagans, les ombrelles et les éventails, cours devant la boutique où la brodeuse se crève les yeux à broder des chiffres sur la neige des draps, cours devant le pédicure barbu qui surveille de sa fenêtre le long trottoir, cours jusqu'au lion de bronze qui garde l'entrée de la villa Fodor. Mais tu vas si vite que je ne te vois plus. T'es-tu sauvé dans l'église où les flammes des cierges palpitent devant la grotte de Lourdes? Dévales-tu la rue Raynouard où, jadis, des chevaux de fiacre prenaient le mors aux dents? Je ne courrai pas après toi, petit revenant de 1908. Il y a trop de changements malheureux dans notre ville pour que je puisse te sourire aussi gaiement que je le voudrais.

Lying awake in the early hours, I sometimes set out on that impossible walk again, and if the fancy takes me, as it once did, to deliver some books to my binder near the rue Raynouard, I hesitate between the rue de l'Annonciation and the rue Jean-Bologne and nearly always choose the latter because of its coal depot, the inhuman beauty of which has the horrifying attraction of a lunar landscape. I wish to gaze at the black pyramids with their sprinkling of silver and at the Babylonian architecture of the stacks of cordwood; I love to breathe in the timeless smell of timber and anthracite and coke and then leave the depot that I have peopled with my sleepwalker's dreams and find myself back in the little street with the village church at the end.

Come with me down this street and meet the ghosts of our earliest years. Run, schoolboy, run, with your satchel bouncing between your shoulderblades – shout, shout for no reason, for the pleasure of being alive, glance quickly into the antique shop, where the grey cat sleeps amid the yataghans, parasols, and fans, run on past the shop where the embroideress is ruining her eyesight stitching initials onto snow-white sheets, run past the bearded chiropodist as he surveys the long pavement from his window, run as far as the bronze lion guarding the entrance to the Villa Fodor. But you're so quick, I've lost sight of you. Have you slipped into the church where the candle flames flicker in front of the grotto of Lourdes? Are you hurtling down the rue Raynouard, where the cab horses needed to be reined in? I'll not go chasing after you, little ghost from 1908. Too much has changed for the worse in our city to let me smile at you as cheerfully as I should like.

Une ville secrète

Paris est une ville dont on pourrait parler au pluriel, comme les Grecs parlaient d'Athènes, car il y a bien des Paris et celui des étrangers n'a que des rapports de surface avec le Paris des Parisiens. L'étranger qui traverse Paris en voiture et va d'un musée à l'autre ne soupçonne pas la présence d'un monde qu'il côtoie sans le voir. A moins d'avoir perdu son temps dans une ville, personne ne saurait prétendre la bien connaître. L'âme d'une grande cité ne se laisse pas si facilement saisir; il faut, pour communiquer avec elle, s'être ennuyé, avoir quelque peu souffert dans les lieux où elle est circonscrite. Sans doute, n'importe qui peut se munir d'un guide et constater la présence de tous les monuments, mais dans les limites mêmes de Paris existe une autre ville aussi difficile d'accès que le fut autrefois Tombouctou.

Cette ville que j'appelle secrète parce que les étrangers n'y pénètrent pas et que je serais tenté d'appeler sacrée parce que ses souffrances nous la rendent plus chère, cette ville, les Parisiens la connaissent si bien et ils trouvent si naturelle son existence qu'ils ne songent pas même à en parler, sauf les romanciers et les poètes dont le rôle est justement de voir comme pour la première fois avec des yeux tout nouveaux ce que nous regardons sans y prendre garde. Encore ces écrivains n'arrivent-ils pas toujours à nous dire clairement ce qu'ils ont découvert. Ils peuvent, par exemple, décrire tous les aspects d'un petit café des environs de la rue de Buci, mais il faudrait la sensibilité particulière d'un Baudelaire ou d'un Proust pour nous en donner ce qu'on appelle aujourd'hui l'atmosphère, pour traduire

A secret city

Paris is a city that might well be spoken of in the plural, as the Greeks used to speak of Athens, for there are many Parises, and the tourists' Paris is only superficially related to the Paris of the Parisians. The foreigner driving through Paris from one museum to another is quite oblivious to the presence of a world he brushes past without seeing. Until you have wasted time in a city, you cannot pretend to know it well. The soul of a big city is not to be grasped so easily; in order to make contact with it, you have to have been bored, you have to have suffered a bit in those places that contain it. Anyone can get hold of a guide and tick off all the monuments, but within the very confines of Paris there is another city as difficult of access as Timbuktu once was.

I call it a secret city because foreigners never enter it, and I am tempted to call it sacred, because its sufferings make it dearer to us. Parisians know it so well and find its existence so natural that they never even dream of talking about it – except for novelists and poets, of course, whose job it is to see as if for the first time, through completely fresh eyes, things to which we pay no attention. Even they do not always succeed in telling us clearly what they have discovered. They may, for instance, describe everything about a little café near the rue de Buci, but it takes the special sensitivity of a Baudelaire or a Proust to give us what is nowadays called its atmosphere, to convey the charm of a certain kind of ugliness, and to render the indefinable sense of companionship that flows from the objects characterizing a place only the inattentive find

le charme d'une certaine laideur et rendre cette indéfinissable bonne camaraderie des objets qui caractérise un endroit banal aux seuls inattentifs: la plante ornée d'un atroce nœud rouge, la banquette de cuir usée et crachant des touffes de crin noir, la table de gros marbre blanc, le sous-main de toile cirée et le porteplume qui a servi à écrire tant de déclarations d'amour et de belles lettres de rupture, et à côté le siphon bleu-pâle, accessoires rituels de la vie de café tel qu'on pourrait les voir dans une toile de Picasso ou de Derain. Et d'une certaine manière, c'est Paris. Tout, dans cette ville, a une qualité inanalysable qui permet de dire sans hésitation 'Ca c'est Paris', quand même ce ne serait qu'une boîte à lait pendue à un bouton de porte, ou un de ces gros balais de bruyère qui chassent les feuilles mortes, en octobre, au bord des trottoirs, avec un bruit d'océan, ou une rangée de bouquins fatigués dans une caisse de bouquiniste, sur les quais, entre le pont Neuf et le pont Royal. Pourquoi il en est ainsi, je n'en sais rien, mais Paris imprime sa marque sur tout ce qui lui appartient. Les touristes sont trop distraits ou disposent de trop peu de temps pour s'en apercevoir, mais le cœur d'un vrai Parisien battra plus vite au souvenir de quelques pots de fleurs sur le bord d'une fenêtre ou d'un refrain populaire que siffle le garçon boucher sur sa bicyclette, si ce Parisien est loin de Paris. Montrez-lui la photographie d'une boulangerie où l'on voit un enfant qui mange son croissant, ou la photographie d'une table ou d'une chaise sur un trottoir avec un garçon à côté, debout dans son tablier blanc et sa serviette sous le bras, il pensera: 'Ceci n'est ni Toulouse, ni Lyon, ni Marseille, bien qu'un observateur superficiel pût s'y tromper. C'est Paris. Bon ou mauvais, ce qui sort d'entre les mains de Paris, c'est Paris, que ce soit une lettre, un morceau de pain, une paire de chaussures ou un poème. Ce que nous donnons au monde, nous ne l'avons emprunté à personne; c'est à nous; on peut nous le prendre, on peut nous le voler, mais l'imiter, non.'

J'ai toujours été fier de Paris parce que Paris est ma ville natale. Chaque promenade que je faisais jadis le long de ses rues semblait créer un nouveau lien, invisible, mais fort et qui m'attachait à ses

ordinary: the plant adorned with a dreadful red ribbon, the worn leather bench spewing out tufts of black horsehair, the solid white marble tabletop, the oilcloth writing pad and the penholder that have served to write so many declarations of love and fine words of parting, and beside them the pale blue siphon – the ritual accessories of café life as portrayed in a painting by Picasso or Derain. And, in a way, that is Paris. Everything in this city has a quality that defies analysis but enables you to say without any hesitation: 'That is Paris' – even if it is only a milk can dangling from a door knob, or one of those coarse brooms sweeping up the leaves at the pavement's edge in October with a sound like the sea, or an array of tired-looking volumes in a bookseller's box on the embankment between the pont Neuf and the pont Royal. Why this should be so I do not know, but Paris sets its seal on everything that belongs to it. The tourists are too distracted or in too much of a hurry to notice it, but the heart of the true Parisian will beat faster, if he is away from Paris, at the memory of a few pots of flowers on a windowsill, or a popular refrain whistled by a butcher's boy as he cycles by. Show him a photograph of a baker's shop with a child eating a croissant, or a photograph of a table or a chair on a pavement with a waiter standing beside them in his white apron, a towel under his arm, and he will think: 'That is neither Toulouse nor Lyon nor Marseille, though the casual observer might be deceived. That is Paris. Good or bad, what Paris produces is Paris, be it a letter, a bit of bread, a pair of socks, or a poem. What we give the world, we have borrowed from no one; it is ours. It may be taken from us, stolen from us, but imitated? – never.'

I have always been proud of Paris because it is the city where I was born. Every walk I have ever taken along its streets has seemed to create a fresh link, invisible yet tenacious, binding me to its very stones. I used to wonder as a child how the mere name of Paris could denote so many different things, so many streets and squares, so many gardens, houses, roofs, chimneys, and above it all the shifting, insubstantial sky that crowns our city; and the more I thought

pierres. Quand j'étais enfant, je me demandais comment il pouvait se faire que le simple nom de Paris désignât tant de choses diverses, tant de rues et de places, tant de jardins, tant de maisons, de toits, de cheminées, et par-dessus tout cela le ciel changeant et léger qui couronne notre ville; et plus j'y pensais, plus il me paraissait étonnant qu'une si grande ville pût tenir dans un nom si court. Je me répétais à moi-même ces deux syllabes qui finissaient par devenir fort mystérieuses dans mon esprit, car, me disais-je, pourquoi l'appelle-t-on ainsi et pas autrement? Mais je croyais qu'à force de répéter ce nom je finirais par découvrir quelque chose, et en fin de compte je ne découvrais rien, sinon que Paris s'appelle Paris.

Aujourd'hui, je me prends quelquefois à remuer dans ma tête des pensées qui ne diffèrent pas beaucoup de celles-là, mais alors qu'il me suffisait de jeter un coup d'œil par la fenêtre pour voir un coin de ma ville natale dont j'aimais déjà les longues rues anciennes, ce bonheur m'est enlevé pour quelque temps, et si je veux revoir Paris, c'est en moi-même que je le retrouve. Chacun de nous porte en lui le Paris de son enfance, de sa jeunesse et de ses rêves, avec une secrète préférence pour le Paris qu'il a logé dans sa mémoire et qui lui paraît plus beau que celui du prochain. Tel Parisien a pris les plus belles églises, son cœur est assez grand pour les loger toutes, et des rangées d'hôtels de la rue de Lille, de la rue de Grenelle et de la rue de Varenne; tel autre affectionne les quais, les jardins qui sommeillent en été derrière les portes cochères des vieilles maisons, ou bien les magasins des antiquaires entre la Seine et le Luxembourg; tel autre songe avec tristesse au petit appartement vieillot d'où il apercevait les tours de Saint-Sulpice et le dôme du Val-de-Grâce, et cet univers lui suffisait …

about it, the more astonishing it seemed to me that so vast a city could fit into so short a name. I used to say the two syllables over and over to myself until they took on a quality of great mystery in my mind, because why, I used to ask myself, was it called that and not something else? But I thought that by repeating the name I should eventually make some discovery, and in the end I discovered nothing, except that Paris is called Paris.

Nowadays I sometimes catch myself turning over in my mind thoughts not so very different from these, but whereas it used to be enough for me just to glance out of the window to see a corner of my native city, of whose long, ancient streets I was already so fond, now that happiness has been taken from me for a while, and if I wish to see Paris again I find it inside myself. Each of us carries within him the Paris of his childhood, his youth, and his dreams, cherishing a secret preference for the Paris that he has tucked away in his memory as being, it seems to him, more beautiful than the next man's. One Parisian will have captured the finest churches, his heart large enough to accommodate them all, and whole rows of town houses in the rue de Lille, the rue de Grenelle, and the rue de Varenne; another's fondness will be for the embankments, the gardens that in summer lie dozing behind the carriage doors of the old houses, or the antique shops between the Seine and the Luxembourg Palace; another will dream sadly of the little old-fashioned flat from which he could see the towers of St Sulpice and the dome of Val-de-Grâce church, and that world was enough for him ...

Le Palais-Royal

Un jour de printemps que des courses m'avaient mené dans les environs du Louvre, je fus chassé par le bruit des rues jusqu'à l'entrée du Palais-Royal qui débouche sur la rue de Beaujolais. C'est un des lieux où rôde on ne saurait dire quoi de mystérieux plus facile à deviner qu'à définir. En avançant sous la voûte sombre, entre les colonnes dont la symétrie, par une bizarrerie d'optique, ne m'était pas apparente, j'eus l'impression de pénétrer dans un bois enchanté et de laisser derrière moi la vie quotidienne, car un des privilèges de Paris, une de ses grâces les plus rares qu'il n'accorde qu'à ceux qui savent y *perdre leur temps*, est de se montrer soudain sous d'insolites aspects, de provoquer à la fois le plaisir de l'inattendu et une subtile inquiétude qui pour un rien tournerait à l'angoisse. Où suis-je donc? Est-ce qu'en revenant sur mes pas je vais retrouver le monde qui m'est familier? Ce sont là des questions qui traversent l'esprit du flâneur s'il est porté, comme moi, à certaines formes de la rêverie, et pendant l'espace d'une ou deux secondes, je connus le léger trouble qu'on ressent alors qu'on croit avoir perdu son chemin. Etait-ce l'éclairage d'un après-midi orageux, ou la solitude fortuite de cet endroit, ou le silence après le grand hourvari des rues et des places? Il me sembla que j'étais au seuil d'un pays nouveau dont le nom ne se lisait dans aucun livre, et où tout ce que nous croyons appartenir au monde matériel devenait, par d'insaisissables opérations, comme l'aspect tangible du monde intérieur; ou plutôt j'eus le sentiment de passer d'un seul coup derrière les coulisses du réel et de surprendre un secret, mais quel secret plus inutile que celui dont on ne pénètre

The Palais-Royal

One spring day when errands had brought me to the vicinity of the Louvre, I was driven by the noise of the streets as far as the north entrance of the Palais-Royal, in the rue de Beaujolais. This is one of those places where there lurks a certain quality of mystery more easily divined than defined. Walking in under the dark vault, between columns whose symmetry, by some quirk of visual perception, was not apparent to me, I had the feeling that I was entering an enchanted forest, leaving everyday life behind me, because one of the privileges of Paris, one of its rarest graces, bestowed only on those who know how to *waste time* there, is suddenly to show itself in unusual guises, arousing both the pleasure of the unexpected and a subtle anxiety that could easily tip over into fear. Where am I? Shall I, when I come to retrace my steps, find myself back in the world I know? Such questions tend to cross the mind of the stroller who is given, as I am, to certain forms of day-dreaming, and for the space of a second or two I experienced the faint distress that comes from thinking you have lost your way. Was it the light of that stormy afternoon, or the fortuitous loneliness of the spot, or the silence after the tumult of the streets and squares? I felt I was on the threshold of a new country whose name figured in no book and where everything we think of as belonging to the material world was by some elusive mechanism becoming, as it were, the tangible aspect of the inner world; or rather I had the feeling of suddenly slipping behind the scenes of reality and coming upon a secret, except what secret could be more futile than one whose meaning escapes you! The fact is, I

pas le sens! Car en vérité je n'aurais su dire en quoi tout me paraissait différent; y avait-il dans tout Paris un coin mieux connu de moi que cet espace borné, ici, par une grille, et là, par d'obscurs magasins qui ressemblaient à des magasins pour fantômes? Ma main frôla une des colonnes blanches et je fis quelques pas en avant. J'avançai moins dans l'espace que dans le souvenir, et moins dans le souvenir de ma propre vie que dans les souvenirs épars de toute une race d'hommes.

Pareil à un halluciné, j'allai placer mon visage entre les barreaux de la grille dont les têtes de pique dorées brillaient contre un ciel menaçant. Ce fut vers ce ciel assombri tournant du gris au lilas que mes regards se dirigèrent. Je l'apercevais entre les petites feuilles d'un vert encore timide et qui palpitaient dans les premiers souffles de l'orage. Un à un, les oiseaux se turent et les bonnes entraînèrent les enfants qui battaient l'air de leur pelle. Bientôt je fus seul à regarder les nuées d'encre qui déferlaient à présent sur les toits dans le solennel murmure du vent. Soudain, à cette minute qui précède le premier coup de tonnerre et où tout paraît attentif au roulement initial, je fus comme arraché à moi-même et livré à une foule invisible. D'innombrables pensées m'envahirent comme un flot qui s'abat sur une grève avec une espèce de tendresse violente. L'âme de toute une ville passait dans les cris, les plaintes et les rires de la tempête qui se levait au-dessus de moi, et mon cœur se mit à battre à l'unisson de cette grande joie pleine de colère et d'alarme. On eût dit qu'au sourd grondement du ciel répondait une voix lointaine venue des profondeurs du temps. J'écoutai, immobile, puis un long trait de feu parcourut le ciel d'un bout à l'autre, et dans le fracas qui suivit presque aussitôt, la pluie fustigea le vieux jardin.

J'entendis avec ravissement ce bruit nombreux aux sonorités étouffées et si bien accordées à la mélancolie des anciens souvenirs; et bientôt monta du sol, me rendant à moi-même, avec cette vaste bénédiction de l'univers que nous ressentons tous à quelque moment de notre vie, l'odeur la plus exquise qui soit au monde,

could not have said what it was that made everything seem different to me: was there a spot in all Paris with which I was more familiar than that space bounded on one side by a wrought-iron gate and on the other by dark shops that might have been shops for ghosts? My hand brushed against one of the white columns, and I took a few paces forward. I was advancing not so much in space as in memory, and not so much in the memory of my own life as in the scattered recollections of a whole race of men.

Like someone experiencing a hallucination, I went over and placed my face between the bars of the gate, the gilded tips of which shone brightly against a threatening sky. It was towards that sombre sky, now turning from grey to lilac, that my gaze was drawn. I could glimpse it between the tiny leaves, still shy in their greenness, that shivered in the first gusts of the storm. One by one the birds fell silent and the nannies dragged away their spade-waving charges. Soon I was the only one left observing the inky clouds as they unfurled above the rooftops amid the solemn murmur of the wind. Suddenly, in that moment that precedes the first clap of thunder, when everything seems to be listening attentively for the initial roll, I was taken out of myself, as it were, and handed over to an invisible crowd. Countless thoughts went flooding through my mind, like a wave crashing on the shore with a sort of violent tenderness. The soul of an entire city entered into the cries, sighs, and guffaws of the storm gathering above my head, and my heart began to beat in unison with that great joy so full of anger and alarm. It was as if the dull rumble of the sky was being answered by a distant voice issuing from the depths of time. I listened, motionless; then a long line of fire split the sky from end to end, and amid the din that almost immediately ensued the rain came lashing down on the ancient garden.

I heard it with delight, that intricate sound whose muffled tones are so aptly tuned to the melancholy of old memories; and soon there rose up from the ground, restoring me to myself with that immense benediction of the universe that we all sense at some time in our lives, the most exquisite smell in the world, at once

à la fois la plus jeune et la plus immémoriale, la plus ténébreuse et la plus innocente, la plus proche des commencements du globe et la plus neuve, celle qui remue au cœur de l'homme le plus de tristesse et le plus de bonheur, le parfum de la terre mouillée.

the freshest and the most immemorial, the most mysterious and the most innocent, the closest to the origins of our planet and the most recent, the smell that moves the heart of man to the greatest sadness and the greatest gladness, the odour of damp earth.

A Notre-Dame

Il est des jours où les choses parlent comme sous le coup d'une inspiration soudaine et nous crient dans un langage à peu près incompréhensible un message dont le sens ne nous apparaît que lorsqu'il est trop tard. On dirait que la matière reçoit le don de vision et prophétise à ses heures, inutilement, car a-t-on jamais écouté un prophète?

Le jeudi saint de 1940, vers la tombée du jour, je me trouvais à Notre-Dame. Un peu en avant du chœur et au milieu de l'allée centrale, quelques-unes des reliques du trésor étaient exposées: les clous, si j'ai bonne mémoire, et, je crois, un fragment de la couronne d'épines. Quatre ou cinq personnes, pas plus, méditaient devant ces objets. Au-dessus de leur tête, une ampoule électrique jetait les rayons de sa dure lumière dans la nuit qui envahissait la nef. Je remarquai, à droite et à gauche du petit autel improvisé, des hommes drapés dans des manteaux blancs, mais si singuliers qu'ils fussent, ils ne retinrent pas d'abord mon attention, car ce que j'entendais m'étonnait beaucoup plus. Tout autour des reliques, en effet, il y avait comme une zone de silence dont il semblait qu'on aurait pu tracer les limites et qui faisait de ces cinq mètres carrés un lieu d'une solitude inexprimable. Cependant, très haut dans le transept, un énorme hourvari. Les vitraux de la grande rose septentrionale avaient été enlevés et une grande bâche les remplaçait dans laquelle le vent s'engouffrait avec une sorte de détonation sourde qui ressemblait à un coup de canon. C'était la dernière rafale de l'hiver et elle secouait l'immense toile grise comme pour

In Notre-Dame

There are days when objects speak as if under the impact of some sudden inspiration. In a language that is virtually incomprehensible they shout a message to us, the meaning of which becomes apparent only when it is too late. It is almost as if matter, receiving the gift of vision, were moved to prophesy – to no avail, of course, for when was a prophet ever listened to?

Around dusk on the Maundy Thursday of 1940 I found myself in Notre-Dame, the Cathedral of Our Lady. Just before the chancel, in the middle of the central gangway, a number of relics from the cathedral treasure were on show: the Nails, if I remember rightly, and I believe a fragment of the Crown of Thorns. Four or five people, no more, were meditating before these things. Above their heads an electric light bulb cast a harsh radiance into the darkness that was beginning to invade the nave. On either side of the little improvised altar I noticed men draped in white cloaks. Odd though these were, however, they did not hold my attention at first because what I was hearing astonished me a great deal more. Around the relics there was a zone of silence that you could almost have defined physically and that made those five square metres a place of inexpressible solitude. Yet high up in the north transept the most tremendous hullabaloo was going on. The stained glass had been removed from the great rose window and replaced by a huge piece of canvas into which the wind would rush with a sort of dull explosion that was like a gun being fired. It was the last gale of winter, and it was shaking the great sheet of grey fabric

la mettre en pièces. Dans les hurlements de la tempête, il semblait impossible de ne pas reconnaître tous les accents de la rage et du désespoir, et j'écoutais ce bruit d'une lugubre magnificence quand je m'aperçus qu'il ne troublait en rien la tranquillité profonde dont s'entourait le petit groupe d'adorateurs. C'est ainsi qu'on voit les arbres courber parfois la tête sous une bourrasque alors qu'à trois ou quatre mètres au-dessous d'eux les fleurs et les feuilles des buissons gardent une immobilité parfaite. La voix immense qui heurtait les voûtes et remplissait la nef d'un fracas de bataille se brisait contre une muraille invisible à quelques pieds du sol et l'on aurait pu entendre à la fois, semblait-il, le bruit léger d'une page qu'on tournait et cette vaste rumeur qui mêlait les cris d'une foule au grondement de chars innombrables.

Ce fut alors que je dirigeai la vue sur les hommes en blanc. Ils étaient assis l'un en face de l'autre, enveloppés dans ces grandes capes dont la couleur me fit songer aux belles églises de Touraine. Chacun portait une grande croix noire brodée sur l'épaule droite, et dans leurs visages empreints d'une grande sévérité je crus lire l'effort de la méditation. Je pensais vaguement aux chevaliers du Saint-Sépulcre quand, tout à coup, l'idée me vint que ces hommes et ces femmes s'étaient rassemblés pour une cérémonie dont le sens leur échappait et qu'en réalité ils veillaient quelqu'un. Ce fut comme si le vent, le crépuscule, les piliers et les voûtes, la cathédrale entière nous criaient à tous un avertissement terrible que nous n'entendions pas. Je sortis presque aussitôt, ne me doutant pas que de cinq ans je ne verrais plus Notre-Dame …

J'y suis retourné l'autre jour. Nous étions en novembre. Un froid glacial tombait sur mes épaules et j'avançai dans la pénombre comme au milieu d'un bois. Il n'est guère de coin de Paris qui ne soit pour moi hanté de souvenirs. Ici je me rappelai l'espèce de frayeur émerveillée qui s'emparait de tout mon être quand, la main dans celle de ma mère, je pénétrais jadis dans la vieille église. Tout enfant est un petit barbare et comme un barbare je demeurais ahuri de tant de grandeur. Aujourd'hui encore, et de quelque amour que

as if to rip it to shreds. The howling of the storm unmistakably conveyed every accent of rage and despair, and as I listened to that noise in all its lugubrious splendour I noticed that it did nothing to disturb the deep tranquillity surrounding the little group of worshippers. In the same way you will sometimes see trees bend their heads beneath a sudden squall while ten or twelve feet below the flowers and leaves of bushes remain perfectly still. The mighty voice crashing about the vaults and filling the nave with the din of battle cut out when it hit an invisible partition a few feet from the ground; it was as if you might have heard, at one and the same time, both the rustle of a page being turned and that monstrous uproar, which combined the shouting of a crowd with the rumble of innumerable tanks.

It was at that point that I directed my gaze at the men in white. They sat facing each other, wrapped in those great capes whose colour put me in mind of the beautiful churches of Touraine. Each wore a large black cross embroidered on his right shoulder, and in their faces, which bore the stamp of great severity, I felt I could detect the effort of meditation. I was musing about Knights of the Holy Sepulchre when the idea suddenly struck me that these men and women had come together for a ceremony whose meaning escaped them, and that in fact they were keeping a vigil. It was as if the wind, the gathering dusk, the pillars and vaults, and the entire cathedral had been shouting a terrible warning to us all, which we could not hear. I left the building almost immediately, having no idea that it would be five years before I saw Notre-Dame again ...

I went back there the other day. The month was November. An icy chill bore down on my shoulders, and I advanced in the half-light as in the middle of a wood. There is scarcely a corner of Paris that is not haunted with memories for me. Here I recalled the sense of awe that would come over my whole being as I entered the ancient church clutching my mother's hand. Every child is a little barbarian, and like a barbarian I was struck dumb by such grandeur. Even today, and loving it as I do, I feel intimidated by

je l'aime, je me sens intimidé par Notre-Dame, par ses profondeurs, par ses échos et par toute cette nuit qu'elle porte en elle.

Arrivé au transept, je levai les yeux vers la rose septentrionale et constatai que le grand haillon gris y était toujours, mais aucun vent ne l'agitait plus et au lieu des vociférations de l'orage j'entendais le murmure beaucoup plus rassurant des chanoines qui lisaient l'office. Je me rappelai alors les chevaliers du Saint-Sépulcre et les femmes agenouillées devant les reliques. Que tout cela me semblait loin, et bizarre la question que je m'étais posée ce jour-là avec effroi: 'Qui veillent-ils donc?'

Mes yeux firent ensuite le tour de l'église et tout à coup s'arrêtèrent. Quelque chose me sauta à la gorge. Ce que je vis, je ne m'attendais pas à le voir, mais je le reconnus aussitôt. Dans le bras méridional du transept, haute et nue, et d'une simplicité bouleversante se dressait la croix de bois destinée aux morts de Buchenwald. Elle était là, attendant et regardant comme les choses savent attendre et regarder. Je restai longtemps près d'elle, ne m'en allant que pour revenir sur mes pas et la considérer de nouveau. Elle était pareille à un grand cri de douleur et d'indignation; sans doute le Moyen Age n'eût-il pas trouvé autre chose pour dire ce que les mots ne pourront jamais dire, et je ne pus me défendre de croire qu'à l'interrogation anxieuse de mars 40 une réponse m'était donnée, en ce mois de novembre 45.

Notre-Dame, by its depths, its echoes, and all the nighttime it harbours within its walls.

Reaching the north transept, I looked up at the rose window. The huge grey cloth was still there, I noted, but with no wind making it flap this time, and in place of the yelling of the storm I could hear the far more reassuring murmur of the canons reciting the office. It was then that I remembered the Knights of the Holy Sepulchre and the women kneeling before the relics. How remote it all seemed to me now, and how odd the question I had asked myself in alarm that day: 'But whose vigil are they keeping?'

My eyes, travelling round the church, suddenly stopped. Something leapt at my throat. The thing I saw I had not expected to see, yet I recognized it immediately. In the south arm of the transept there stood, tall, bare, and overwhelming in its simplicity, the wooden cross dedicated to those who had died in Buchenwald. There it was, waiting and watching in the way objects have the ability to wait and watch. I stood near it for some time, turning away only to retrace my steps and go back and look at it again. It was like a great cry of pain and indignation; doubtless the Middle Ages would have found no other way of saying what words will never be capable of saying, and I could not help thinking that my anxious question of March 1940 had, on this November day in 1945, received an answer.

Paris des escaliers

Du plus loin qu'il me souvienne, je crois voir un escalier dont parlait quelquefois ma mère. L'histoire qu'elle nous racontait me glaçait toujours de la même horreur, mais la narratrice se figurait que je ne comprenais pas parce qu'elle s'exprimait en anglais. Elle avait passé sa jeunesse à Savannah, en Georgie, dans une charmante maison de style colonial d'où l'on voyait des sycomores ombrageant une grande place. Dans les Etats du Sud, le crépuscule est bref, la nuit tombe comme un rideau noir, saluée, au plus chaud de l'été, par le chant continu des rainettes. L'ombre est-elle plus épaisse qu'ailleurs en cette partie du monde? Je le croirais. Elle semble, en tout cas, pleine de maléfices. Pour monter du salon à sa chambre (après le bruit des voix, des rires, de la valse, j'imagine sans peine le silence hanté par ce chant cristallin qui forme comme un tissu sonore tendu entre le coucher et le lever du soleil), ma mère prenait un petit escalier assez étroit, trop étroit pour que deux personnes pussent y monter de front, et là, disait-elle, il lui semblait toujours que quelqu'un la suivait en marmonnant à son oreille. Elle ajoutait, non pas en guise d'éclaircissement, mais soucieuse malgré tout d'indiquer une relation possible de cause à effet: 'La maison était construite sur l'emplacement d'une vieille prison où l'on avait pendu pas mal de criminels.'

Je tirais de ce récit les conclusions épouvantées qui me rendaient suspects tous les escaliers du monde et jusqu'à l'honnête escalier qui menait à notre appartement de la rue de Passy; pour tout dire, je ne me sentais brave, en cet endroit, que là où le vitrage colorié

Stairways and steps

As far back as I remember, I believe I see a staircase that my mother talked about occasionally. The story she used to tell us always froze me with the same sense of horror, but the narrator imagined I did not understand because she was speaking in English. She had spent her youth in Savannah, Georgia, in a delightful colonial-style house that commanded a view of sycamore trees shading a large square. In the Southern states, after a brief twilight, night falls like a black curtain, heralded, at the height of summer, by the sustained singing of tree frogs. Is the darkness deeper in that part of the world than elsewhere? I could almost think it was. Certainly it would appear to teem with evil spells. To get from the drawing-room to her bedroom (after the voices, the laughter, and the dancing I can readily imagine the silence, haunted by that crystalline song weaving as it were a fabric of sound that was stretched taut between sunset and sunrise) my mother used a little, narrow staircase, too narrow for a couple to climb side by side, and there, she said, she always had the feeling someone was following her, muttering in her ear. She used to add, not as an explanation, but with a certain concern, all the same, to indicate a possible link between cause and effect: 'The house stood on the site of an old penitentiary, where a good many criminals had been hanged.'

From this story I drew the terrified conclusions that caused me to be wary of all staircases everywhere – even the inoffensive one that led up to our flat in the rue de Passy. The fact is, I felt brave only where the coloured glass of a window shed its light on the red

d'une fenêtre laissait tomber la lumière sur le tapis rouge et les tringles de cuivre, mais dans le coin obscur où l'escalier faisait un retour sur lui-même je courais avec tous les suppliciés de la prison américaine à mes trousses.

Avec le temps, ces terreurs enfantines s'assagirent, mais il en resta quelque chose, et je crois qu'aujourd'hui encore l'escalier le plus banal n'est pas tout à fait sans mystère à mes yeux. Vu d'une certaine façon, il prolonge la rue ou la route et comme elles il est chargé de toutes les pensées de l'homme qui va vers son but. N'a-t-on pas remarqué l'air absorbé des gens qui montent d'étage en étage? Que de résolutions prises, que de questions agitées dont la réponse attend derrière telle porte qui va s'ouvrir tout à l'heure! C'est ici, sur ces marches, le lieu et le moment de se décider, la dernière minute de réflexion avant le geste définitif. Aussi dirait-on qu'il traîne dans certaines de ces grandes cages circulaires un peu des rêves qu'elles ont abrités et comme un souvenir de ces méditations où l'amour, la convoitise et l'ennui se disputèrent le cœur de tous ces passants inconnus.

Paris est une ville d'escaliers qui provoquent l'imagination. Je ne pense pas à ces vieux hôtels, dont les montées orgueilleuses sont comme de nobles discours où chaque palier marque une halte entre deux périodes, mais à ces escaliers bourgeois, riches de secrets, de brouilles, de calculs, au point qu'un romancier ne saisit point la rampe sans qu'un personnage lui vienne souffler un mot et montrer un coin de son visage. Je connais tel escalier en spirale du quartier du Temple où l'idée d'une poursuite se présente irrésist-iblement à l'esprit. Dans tel autre, étroit et contourné, la question se pose de savoir si un cercueil passerait sans heurter les parois et à quelles patientes manœuvres il conviendrait de se livrer pour ne pas *déranger* l'occupant de la longue boîte noire.

Que de fois, dans un passage obscur du quartier de la Bourse, ne me suis-je pas arrêté au bas d'un escalier dont la spirale fastueuse s'enroule avec une hautaine nonchalance et part pour un voyage dans les ténèbres! La pomme de cuivre, la rampe de chêne et les

carpet and the brass stair rods; in the dark corner where the staircase turned back on itself I used to run with all the torture victims of that American prison on my tail.

In time these childish terrors subsided, but something of them remained, and I believe that even today the most ordinary flight of stairs is not wholly without mystery in my eyes. A staircase, after all, may be seen as an extension of the street or the road, and like them it is charged with all the thoughts of the man drawing near to his destination. Have you never noticed how absorbed people look as they climb from floor to floor? So many resolutions reached, so many anxious questions to which the answers lie in wait behind the door that is about to open! Here on the stairs is the time and the place for making up your mind, that final moment of reflection before you take the plunge. As a result there appears to linger, in some of those great circular stairwells, a residue of the dreams that they have sheltered, a memory, as it were, of the meditations in which love, lust, and world-weariness fought for the hearts of all the nameless people who ever passed that way.

Paris is a city of staircases that challenge the imagination. I am not thinking of the old mansions, whose proud flights are like elegant speeches in which each landing marks a pause between periods; I have in mind those bourgeois staircases so replete with intrigues, quarrels, and ulterior motives that a novelist cannot even grasp the banister without some character whispering in his ear and granting him a glimpse of a face. I know one particular spiral staircase in the Temple quarter where the idea of a chase springs irresistibly to mind. Another one, narrow and twisting, makes you wonder whether a coffin would pass without striking the walls and what patient manoeuvres it would be appropriate to perform in order to avoid *disturbing* the occupant of the long black box.

The number of times that, slipping through some dark passage near the Stock Exchange, I have stopped at the foot of a staircase whose sumptuous spiral unwinds with haughty nonchalance as it climbs into the darkness! The brass knob, oak banister, and treads

marches grises de poussière se parent à mes yeux d'une beauté de roman qui me suit longtemps après que j'ai retrouvé la rue; je puis me figurer quelques-uns des personnages admirables que la vie, avec son insolente prodigalité de grand écrivain, a fait monter et descendre dans ce puits d'ombre, pour le plaisir, semble-t-il, d'étaler ses dons et de narguer ses imitateurs. Un escalier pour Lautréamont…

Mais, si ces escaliers d'immeuble irritent la curiosité, quelle apaisante mélancolie versent dans l'âme du flâneur les marches de pierre qui l'invitent à longer les bords de la Seine et à se perdre dans la contemplation de ses eaux noires! C'est là, sur le port, qu'il fait bon promener ses rêves et jeter en arrière de ces grands coups d'œil inutiles qui mesurent le temps parcouru. La gravité particulière à ce lieu a quelque chose qui retient secrètement l'homme enclin aux méditations vagabondes et dont le cœur se nourrit de regrets. Il lui semble en remontant les marches, qu'il a fait provision de souvenirs et qu'il s'est enrichi d'une tristesse nouvelle.

Un autre affectionnera les escaliers paresseux qui s'accrochent aux flancs de Montmartre et dont les degrés eux-mêmes paraissent las d'une perpétuelle ascension. Pour ma part, je ne me consolerai pas d'avoir vu démolir le charmant escalier qui s'appuyait au cimetière de Passy et descendait pensivement jusqu'à la place du Trocadéro. La grande avenue banale qui l'a jeté à bas et semble avoir fait sa trouée à coups de char d'assaut ne compense en rien la disparition d'un point de Paris, mais il est agréable de se souvenir de ces vieilles pierres et je crois les voir assez fidèlement par le secours de ma mémoire: d'un côté, il y avait la haute muraille sombre et nue, couronnée de cyprès emphatiques, de l'autre, la vue plongeait entre les arbres jusqu'au cœur d'un fouillis de verdure. La nuit, un réverbère d'ancienne mode couchait sur les longues marches basses la silhouette d'un promeneur attardé qui ne se résignait pas à aller dormir et qui entendait sonner des heures indues à quelque horloge du voisinage. Morts et vivants, tout dormait. Et le silence qui régnait était un grand silence de province.

grey with dust assume a fictional beauty in my eyes that remains with me long after I have regained the street; I can picture some of the wonderful characters that life, with the brazen prodigality of the great writer, has had ascend and descend that well of shadow – for the pleasure, it would seem, of parading its gifts and cocking a snook at its imitators. A staircase for Lautréamont…

But if these interior staircases tease one's curiosity, what soothing melancholy is poured into the stroller's heart by the flights of stone steps inviting him down to the banks of the Seine to loaf there, lost in contemplation of its dark waters! It is a good place, the lower embankment, to take your dreams for a walk and cast behind you those grand, futile glances that measure the time you have travelled. Something about its peculiar gravity exerts a secret hold on the kind of man who is given to roving meditations and whose heart feeds on regrets. As he climbs back up the steps, it is with the feeling that he has laid in a store of memories and is richer by a fresh sadness.

Another person will have a fondness for the lazy flights of steps that cling to the flanks of Montmartre, their very treads apparently weary of forever climbing. I know I shall never get over having witnessed the demolition of the delightful flight of steps that backed onto Passy cemetery and descended thoughtfully towards the Trocadero. The broad, humdrum avenue that brought about their downfall and that looks as if it battered its way through like a tank is no recompense for the disappearance of a bit of Paris, but it is a pleasure to recall those ancient stones, and I reckon I picture them pretty faithfully with the aid of memory: on the one side there was the tall, dark, bare wall crowned by emphatic cypresses; on the other the eye dived between the trees to lodge in a thicket of greenery. At night an old-fashioned streetlamp cast a silhouette on the long, low steps, the silhouette of someone out walking late, unable to resign himself to going to bed, hearing unseemly hours chime from a neighbouring clock. Everyone, the dead and the living, was asleep. And the silence that reigned was a deep, provincial silence.

Le Val-de-Grâce

L'autre soir, je me promenais du côté de la rue des Feuillantines et le nom du Val-de-Grâce travaillait en moi. Quand on remonte la rue Saint-Jacques, à un endroit elle se resserre et devient la rue de province qu'elle voudrait être. Si la nuit est claire, si les ombres sont bien nettes et bien blanche la lumière de la lune, il arrive un moment où le flâneur le mieux informé de tout le mystère de sa ville s'arrête et regarde en silence. Paris ne se livre guère aux gens pressés, je l'ai déjà dit, il appartient aux rêveurs, à ceux qui savent s'amuser dans les rues sans question de temps alors que d'urgentes besognes les réclament ailleurs; aussi leur récompense est-elle de voir ce que d'autres ne verront jamais. Paris a de plus cette particularité de se montrer la nuit mieux qu'il ne le fait le jour. On dirait qu'il attend que tout le monde soit couché. En plein soleil, il tient le discours de toutes les capitales anciennes, avec des effets oratoires qui étonnent: telle avenue est une longue période conduite avec fermeté à un terme qu'on prévoyait sans le croire tout à fait possible; telle place est un lieu commun renouvelé avec l'apparente facilité du génie. Mais dans l'ombre Paris est tout autre, et s'il parle, c'est à lui-même que s'adresse son ténébreux discours. Je n'ai pas la prétention d'y entendre grandchose, mais je sais que, lorsque l'on arrive par la rue Saint-Jacques à la petite place qui s'étend en arc de cercle devant le Val-de-Grâce, on ne peut faire que s'arrêter tout à coup, si les rayons de la lune tombent droit sur le dôme de l'église. Cela, je l'ai vu l'autre nuit. Comme un vaste écran noir, la façade restait dans l'obscurité avec ses frontons, ses colonnes et le ruban froncé de ses

Val-de-Grâce church

The other evening I was walking in the vicinity of the rue des Feuil-lantines and the name Val-de-Grâce – 'Valley of Grace' – was alive in my mind. As you climb the rue Saint-Jacques, it narrows at one point and becomes the provincial street it would like to be. If the night is a clear one, and if the shadows are sharp and the moonlight good and white, there comes a moment when the best-informed stroller, as far as all the mystery of his city is concerned, stops and stares in silence. Paris, as I have said, is loath to surrender itself to people who are in a hurry; it belongs to the dreamers, to those capable of amusing themselves in its streets without regard to time when urgent busi-ness requires their presence elsewhere; consequently their reward is to see what others will never see. Paris has the further character-istic of revealing itself better at night than it does in the daytime. It seems to wait until everyone is asleep. In the full light of day it holds forth like any other ancient capital, using some startling oratorical effects: a particular avenue will be a long sentence brought firmly to a conclusion that, while you saw it coming, you never quite believed possible; a square will be a commonplace revived with the apparent facility of genius. In the dark, however, Paris is quite different, and if it speaks it is to itself that its darkly mysterious words are addressed. I cannot claim to hear many of them, but I do know that, as you come up the rue Saint-Jacques and enter the little square that forms an apron in front of Val-de-Grâce church, you involuntarily stop in your tracks if the moon is shining straight down onto the dome of the building. I saw that the other night. Like a huge black screen

corniches, tous les falbalas d'un style merveilleusement suranné, tandis qu'en arrière de ce morceau d'éloquence une espèce de miracle avait lieu: la coupole s'évanouissait dans la lumière qui semblait en changer la substance. C'était comme si ce dôme s'était mué en verre et l'on s'attendait presque à voir les étoiles briller à travers cette architecture de songe.

J'ai toujours pensé qu'en observant les choses avec beaucoup d'attention et de persévérance, on finit par leur ravir un peu de leurs secrets et par leur faire dire ce qu'elles ont le plus à cœur de garder pour elles. Un simple caillou a son mystère: la matière est une taciturne doublée d'une bavarde. Rivé donc sur place par la beauté de ce dôme aérien, je le voyais reculer au fond d'un ciel transparent et revêtir tout à coup un air de splendeur presque orientale; puis il grandit jusqu'à remplir la voûte nocturne et, devenu d'un noir d'encre, par le subit passage de nuées, offrit à ma vue les majestueux contours d'une basilique romaine. La gamme de ces transformations appelait irrésistiblement l'idée d'une sorte de musique que seul l'esprit pouvait saisir. Je demeurai ému de tout ce qui m'était donné d'un seul coup par la grâce d'un peu de lumière et la pensée me vint presque aussitôt que peut-être ce que je voyais ne durerait pas, que d'autres églises, n'ayant que leur simple beauté pour toute défense, s'étaient écroulées tristement sous les bombes et qu'une nuit, une nuit peut-être aussi pure que celle-ci, je ne sais quel engin d'une barbarie savante broierait cette coupole, comme une coquille d'œuf; et l'église alors murmura distinctement cette parole qui livre un peu du secret des pierres d'autrefois: 'Plus je suis menacée, plus je suis belle.'

the façade was left in darkness with its pediments, its columns, and the gathered ribbon of its cornices, all the furbelows of a wonderfully antiquated style, while behind this piece of eloquence a kind of miracle was taking place: the dome disappeared in the light, which seemed to change its substance. It was as if it had been turned to glass, and you half expected to see the stars shining through that dream-like architecture.

I have always thought that by observing things with a great deal of attention and perseverance you eventually wrest some of their secrets from them, making them utter what they would most like to keep to themselves. An ordinary pebble possesses its mystery: matter is taciturn when it is not being garrulous. Glued to the spot, then, by the beauty of that aerial dome, I watched it withdraw into the depths of a transparent sky and suddenly assume an air of almost oriental splendour; after that it grew until it filled the whole vault of the night sky and, plunged abruptly into inky blackness by some passing clouds, presented me with the majestic outlines of a Roman basilica. The gamut of these changes irresistibly called to mind the idea of a kind of music that only the mind could grasp. I was deeply moved by all that had been given me at once, thanks to a little bit of light, and the thought occurred to me almost immediately that perhaps what I was seeing would not last, that other churches, with no defence but their beauty, had regrettably collapsed beneath the bombs and that one night, perhaps a night as pure as this one, some missile of ingenious barbarity would smash this dome like an eggshell; and at that point the church quietly articulated these words, which tell us something of the secret of old buildings: 'The worse I am threatened, the lovelier I become.'

La vilaine école

C'est le secret des grandes villes d'offrir des promenades dont le charme est souvent inexplicable, et l'on aura beau me dire que mon contentement est fait de ce que les maisons sont belles et les cours profondes, et vieilles les pierres, il y a autre chose à quoi les mots ne peuvent que faire allusion: une certaine légèreté de cœur que donne la vue d'un arbre auprès d'un toit, ou dans une rue ensoleillée, la subite fraîcheur d'une voûte obscure sous les croisées dédaigneuses d'un hôtel d'autrefois. Ainsi tout prétexte m'est bon pour errer dans la merveilleuse ville de province qui s'étend des grilles du Luxembourg au pont des Saints-Pères et que dominent le beffroi de Saint-Germain-des-Prés et les tours de Saint-Sulpice; et j'en pourrais dire ce que le vieux Samuel Johnson disait à peu près de Londres, à savoir que lorsqu'on est las de ses rues, on est las de la vie, mais depuis plusieurs mois, je ne me promène plus sans inquiétude de ce côté.

Qu'après tant d'années destructrices, Paris soit encore debout, il est devenu banal de dire que c'est là une sorte de miracle, un miracle dont nous nous réjouissons tous les jours. Mais si la beauté de Paris a pu échapper aux guerres, admirons qu'elle ne puisse rien contre la pioche des Parisiens eux-mêmes quand ils se mettent en tête de démolir, ni contre la bizarrerie de leurs architectes quand on ne les surveille pas! Peu m'importe de savoir qui a élevé l'étrange abomination qu'on peut voir au coin de la rue des Saint-Pères et de la rue Jacob, ni pourquoi elle est là, car il faut lui rendre cette justice qu'elle est d'une laideur assez éloquente pour frapper d'inutilité

The ugly school

It is the secret of big cities to offer walks whose charm often defies explanation, and don't go telling me that my satisfaction stems from the houses being beautiful, the gardens and courtyards deep, and the stones ancient: there is something else to which words can only allude, a certain lightness of heart at the sight of a tree beside a roof, or in a sunny street the sudden coolness of a dark archway beneath the haughty casements of a former mansion. So any excuse will do when I feel like wandering round the marvellous provincial town that extends from the railings of the Luxembourg Palace to the pont des Saints-Pères and is overlooked by the belfry of St Germain-des-Prés and the towers of St Sulpice. Paraphrasing what the elderly Samuel Johnson said of London, I might say that when a man is tired of its streets he is tired of life. However, for some months now I have not walked that way without a feeling of unease.

It has become somewhat trite, nowadays, to say that after so many years of destruction it is a kind of miracle that Paris is still standing, a miracle we thrill to every day. But if the beauty of Paris has survived wars, how extraordinary that it can do nothing against the pickaxes of the Parisians themselves when they make up their minds to demolish something, nor against the vagaries of their architects when left to their own devices! I care neither who built the strange abomination that can be seen at the corner of the rue des Saints-Pères and the rue Jacob nor what it is doing there, for we must, in fairness, allow that its hideousness speaks for itself in a way

toutes les explications possibles. Le fait est qu'elle est là, au cœur d'un des plus beaux quartiers de la ville qui s'enorgueillit d'être la plus belle ville du monde, et le scandale est grand. La construction de cette école de médecine ne le cède en rien ni en lourdeur ni en tristesse à aucun des blockhaus que l'on a construits pendant la guerre, et elle mériterait que, modifiant le trait lancé jadis à Rome contre les Barberini, on inscrivît au-dessus de la porte: 'Ce que ne firent point les Barbares, des Parisiens l'ont fait.'

that renders all comment superfluous. The fact is, there it stands, at the heart of one of the loveliest quarters of what prides itself on being the most beautiful city in the world, and that is an outrage. The new School of Medicine is every bit as massive and every bit as dismal as any of the blockhouses erected during the war, and it deserves to have inscribed above its doorway, in a version of the gibe once aimed at the Barberini family in Rome, 'What the Barbarians left undone, Parisians have accomplished.'

Le cloître des Billettes

A quelques pas de l'Hôtel de Ville, il y a un temple luthérien auquel s'appuie une petite maison d'aspect benoît et qui a l'air de ne rien cacher derrière ses murs. J'ai souvent regardé la façade du temple qui est d'une étrange sévérité et l'autre jour, à ma honte soit dit, j'ai pour la première fois poussé la porte de la maison. De surprise, je suis demeuré immobile, puis, faisant quelques pas, j'ai quitté le XXe siècle pour avancer dans le XVe. Avec une charmante sournoiserie de prestidigitateur, Paris avait tiré comme de sa manche un petit cloître ogival où j'errai avec ravissement.

A vrai dire, il n'était guère plus grand qu'une salle de bal, mais pas une arcade n'y manquait et j'en eusse fait plusieurs fois le tour, n'eût été un sérieux obstacle. Cet obstacle était la loge qui abrite la concierge du temple, peut-être la seule loge de tout Paris où la concierge fasse son ménage sous des voûtes du temps de Charles VII. La seule aussi où cette même concierge, que j'envie en la circonstance, puisse lever les yeux du magazine qu'elle parcourt et promener la vue d'un pilier gothique à un autre. Les remarque-t-elle? Sans doute elle constate leur présence, mais arrive-t-il jamais un moment où elle les voit? J'ai sur elle l'avantage de regarder ces pierres pour la première fois, alors qu'elle les a devant les yeux du matin au soir; mais lui parlent-ils jamais, ces piliers d'une inébranlable fidélité qui se retrouvent chaque jour au rendez-vous qu'elle leur donne tacitement sans y réfléchir et qui demeurent à leur poste jusqu'à ce qu'elle ait fermé ses paupières? Quant à dire ce qu'ils font ensuite, nous n'en savons rien d'une façon certaine,

The cloister of Les Billettes

A few minutes' walk from the Hôtel de Ville there is a Lutheran church with, abutting on it, a bland little building apparently hiding nothing within its walls. I have often looked at the façade of the church, which is curiously severe, and the other day, as I admit to my shame, I pushed open the door of the house next door for the first time. Surprise rooted me to the spot; then, taking a few paces forward, I walked out of the twentieth century and into the fifteenth. With the charming duplicity of the conjuror, Paris had pulled from its sleeve, as it were, a little Gothic cloister, where I wandered about in high delight.

It was hardly bigger than a ballroom, in fact. But not a single arch was missing, and I should have walked round it several times but for a serious obstacle. That obstacle was the cottage for the church caretaker, possibly the only lodge in Paris where the concierge keeps house beneath vaults dating from the reign of Charles VII. The only one, moreover, where that same concierge, who in this instance enjoys my envy, can look up from the magazine she is skimming through and run her eye over one Gothic pillar after another. Does she notice them? She is aware of their presence, no doubt, but does there ever come a moment when she sees them? I have this advantage over her, that I am looking at these stones for the first time, whereas she has them in front of her all day long; but do they ever speak to her, these unshakeably loyal pillars that each day keep the appointment she tacitly, unwittingly gives them and then stay at their posts until she closes her eyes? As to saying what they do after

mais je me demande si cette femme dort du même sommeil que nous: voit-elle des processions de robes noires passer à travers les murs de sa loge et ramène-t-elle sa couverture sur une oreille épouvantée par le murmure des hymnes? A bien y réfléchir je pense que non. Par un de ces beaux jours d'avril où Paris sent déjà les premières poussières de l'été, je me suis tenu un moment dans un angle du cloître avec un chaperon imaginaire sur la tête et un cœur de Moyen Age battant sous mon pourpoint de drap épinard, car pour des raisons diverses, j'ai la nostalgie de cette époque où je crois que demeurait encore au plus secret de l'homme une paix que nous avons perdue, et le lieu dont je parle est de ceux où cette paix intérieure semble aussi naturellement chez elle que dans les phrases de l'*Imitation*.

Voici donc ce petit cloître qui nous donne son silence à lui, son silence du XVe siècle, et ses arcades pensives présentent assez bien l'image d'une âme qui se replie sur elle-même et se recueille comme nous ne savons plus le faire. J'en arrive là, en effet, et retrouve mon point de départ en visitant par le souvenir ce vestige du grand Paris médiéval. L'après-midi touchait à sa fin; il y avait dans ces murs, dans l'ombre des piliers massifs, un peu du trésor qu'on nous arrache à toute heure du jour et dont la privation définitive ferait périr en nous ce que nous possédons encore de meilleur; il y avait le silence, un silence non pas troublé, mais rendu plus profond par le bruit égal et cristallin d'une goutte d'eau tombant dans un baquet, non loin d'un arbuste qui tendait vers le ciel ses petites feuilles toutes neuves et transparentes; et sur le rebord de la fenêtre par laquelle la concierge jetait parfois un coup d'œil de mon côté, un chat blanc, tacheté de noir, son masque posé de travers sur un visage d'assassin, surveillait avec une patience féroce un pigeon gris et mauve qui roucoulait en sourdine, innocemment, sous les branches.

that, we have no way of knowing for certain, but I wonder whether that woman sleeps the same sort of sleep as we do: does she witness processions of black robes passing through her bedroom walls, and does she pull up the bedclothes over ears terrified by the murmur of hymns? I think not, all things considered. On one of those splendid April days when Paris already smells of the first of summer's dust, I stood for a moment in a corner of the cloister wearing an imaginary hood and with a medieval heart beating beneath my doublet of dark green cloth, because for a variety of reasons I am nostalgic for a period when I believe man still, in the deepest part of his being, possessed a peace we have lost, and the place I am talking about is one of those where that inner peace seems as naturally at home as in the pages of Thomas à Kempis.

So there it is, this little cloister that gives us its peculiar silence, its fifteenth-century silence, and whose pensive arcades present a very fair picture of a soul withdrawing into itself and meditating in a way we have forgotten how to do. I am getting there, actually, and I remind myself of my starting-point by revisiting, in memory, this remnant of the great medieval city of Paris. The afternoon was drawing to a close; in those walls, in the shadow of those massive pillars, there was a little of the treasure that is being wrested from us every hour of the day, complete deprival of which would kill off the best we still have within us; there was silence, a silence not disturbed but made deeper by the steady, crystalline sound of water dripping into a tub. The tub stood beside a bush that held its tiny leaves, all fresh and translucent, up towards the sky; and on the sill of the window through which the concierge cast the occasional glance in my direction, a white cat with black spots, its mask set aslant on the face of a killer, kept watch, with ferocious patience, on a mauve and grey pigeon that was quietly, innocently, cooing among the branches.

Le Trocadéro parle

S'il est vrai qu'on a démoli le Trocadéro sans que l'ordre exprès en ait été donné, il faut croire que le colosse a été vaincu par la seule puissance du mépris général et que la pensée de plusieurs millions d'hommes peut être aussi forte que la signature d'un ministre. Pour ma part, j'ai applaudi aux premiers coups de pioche que donnaient dans l'azur des ouvriers minuscules, j'ai salué la chute des balustrades façonnières et de toutes les abominations mauresques qui déshonoraient le ciel de Chaillot. Calors que le vrai Trocadéro m'a parlé.

Au point où j'en suis, me dit-il, quelle différence entre moi et les plus vaniteuses ruines de l'Histoire? Par une nuit sans lune, le temple de Bel paraissait-il plus ténébreux ou plus maléfique lorsque les soudards de Xerxès en eurent renversé les colonnes? Sois honnête. Je suis un peu le temple du dieu poisson des Philistins après l'accès de rage du héros juif, et le temple de Jérusalem devait me ressembler, en plus petit, quand l'Eternel fatigué l'eut abandonné à la fureur des Gentils. Allons, Titus n'a pas vu autre chose que ce que tu vois, de grands pans de murs horrifiés, des piliers en détresse, des escaliers qui montent dans le vide, une espèce de bousculade immobile des pierres et cet affolement muet des choses qui se sentent frappées: aveugle qui répétais que je n'étais pas beau!

Au fond, c'est toi qui m'as tué. Mais oui! Tu as fait chorus avec trop d'étourdis. Je cède la place à mon épouvantable successeur: il sera blanc et banal comme un bloc de sucre et tu regretteras mes briques, mes fanfreluches de bazar, mes minarets. Et puis tu finiras bien par te souvenir

The Trocadero speaks

If it is true that the old Trocadero Palace was demolished without a specific order having been issued, we have to accept that the giant was overthrown by the power of universal contempt alone and that the minds of several million people can be as mighty as a minister's signature. I certainly applauded the first pickaxe blows dealt by tiny workers high up in the blue; I welcomed the collapse of those fussy balustrades and all the Moorish abominations that disgraced the Chaillot skyline. That was when the real Trocadero spoke to me.

The way I am now [it told me], what is the difference between me and the most vainglorious ruins in History? Did the Temple of Baal, on a moonless night, look any more shadowy, any more evil after Xerxes' ruffianly crew had toppled its columns? Be honest, now. I'm not unlike the temple of the fish god of the Philistines following the Jewish hero's fit of rage, and the Temple of Jerusalem must have borne a certain resemblance to me, on a smaller scale, when the Everlasting Lord had wearily abandoned it to the fury of the Gentiles. Admit it, Titus saw nothing different from what you are seeing – huge, horrified expanses of wall, anguished pillars, stairways climbing into emptiness, a kind of motionless jostling of stones, and that mute panic of things that know they have been struck. Are you blind, that you kept saying I was not beautiful?

It was you that killed me, when all's said and done. Oh yes it was! You went along with too many fools. I am making way for my dreadful successor, who will be white and plain, like a lump of sugar. Then you will miss my bricks, my cheap frills and flounces, my minarets. And eventually

des distributions de prix que j'abritais dans mon ventre, des gloires en plâtre doré, des oasis de palmes, des professeurs, des discours dont les échos vigoureux se lançaient les paroles comme des balles. En entendant s'effondrer ce qui reste de moi, dis-toi bien, petit, que le cordon de dynamite n'était pas mal placé, et qu'avec le Trocadéro diffamé, c'est ton enfance, elle-même, qui saute.

Cependant, la nuit, avec son art consommé des généralisations flatteuses, nous montre un Trocadéro que beaucoup n'oublieront jamais. Ce que sait faire le ciel de Paris avec un rien de brouillard et le degré d'obscurité nécessaire m'a toujours confondu de surprise. Il est une heure du crépuscule d'hiver où la ville semble livrée aux extravagances délicieuses d'un illusionniste qui voudrait nous faire prendre ce qui est pour ce qui n'est pas et créer dans l'esprit du promeneur de riches, de féériques malentendus. Je me suis trouvé hier soir devant un prodigieux amas d'ombre, là où mon œil cherchait une ruine médiocre. Les tours découronnées s'enveloppaient d'une brume légère où les lumières de la ville jetaient ce rose inquiétant, ce reflet d'incendie et de fin du monde qui nimbe les capitales. Comme un cratère, la partie supérieure du monument béait et un large torrent de gravats s'échappait de la salle des fêtes, mais grâce à la magie nocturne, toute vulgarité s'effaçait, et ce qui de jour n'était quentreprise de démolition revêtait à présent cet air théâtral qui est comme la parure des grandes catastrophes… J'imagine que les Tuileries incendiées avaient cet aspect, lorsque les cendres en furent refroidies.

you will recall the prize-givings I accommodated within my bowels, the gilded plaster haloes, the oases of palm trees, the professors, the speeches whose powerful echoes hurled words about like bullets. As you hear what is left of me come crashing down, just you tell yourself, little man, that the charges were pretty well laid and that, along with the defamed Trocadero, this is your childhood being blown up.

Meanwhile night, that master of the flattering generalization, presents us with a Trocadero that many will never forget. I am consistently amazed by what the Paris sky can do with a hint of fog and the requisite degree of darkness. There is a point during winter's twilight when the city seems to be given over to the charming nonsense of an illusionist, who would have us take what is for what is not, seeking to create exuberant, enchanting misunderstandings in the mind of the strolling observer. Last night I found myself facing a prodigious mass of shadow where my eye had expected an indifferent ruin. The uncapped towers were draped in a thin mist in which the lights of the city cast that disturbing pinkness, that fiery, end-of-the-world glow that suffuses all big cities. The upper part of the monument lay wide open, like a crater, and a broad torrent of rubble spilled out from the great hall. Thanks to the magic of night, however, any vulgarity was obliterated, and what by day was simply a demolition site now assumed the theatrical air that is, so to speak, the panoply of major catastrophes ... I imagine the burnt-out Tuileries Palace looked like that, once the ashes had cooled.

Musées, rues, saisons, visages

Au musée de l'Homme. Grand plaisir à retrouver Namba, la déesse de la maternité. Avec son bec de perroquet au bout duquel pend un petit carré d'étoffe et son énorme manteau de paille, elle est proprement terrifiante. Je l'ai imaginée portée en triomphe au son de *la Marseillaise* ou du *Star Spangled Banner*; cela lui donnerait un aspect encore plus singulier... Regardé aussi le joyeux costume qui se porte, je ne sais plus où, aux cérémonies de la circoncision. Plus loin, un admirable tambour de l'Oubangui, deux grandes surfaces de bois qui se rejoignent par le haut pour se terminer en tête de buffle d'une délicatesse extrême avec de très belles cornes merveilleusement incurvées. En regardant par la fenêtre, par-dessus les arbres du Trocadéro, la tour Eiffel prenait un air insolite...

D'une pièce tout en fenêtres, rue du Louvre, au dernier étage d'un grand journal du soir où j'ai passé un moment, j'ai découvert la vue la plus admirable que je connaisse des vieux toits de Paris: rue Montorgueil, rue d'Aboukir, rue de Cléry... Il pleuvait à verse et la lumière s'évanouissait dans les grands rayons argentés de ce déluge. Toutes ces maisons des XVIIe et XVIIIe siècles, avec leurs chapeaux de tuiles brunes, combien de temps dureront-elles encore?

Au musée des Arts et Métiers. Grande salle pleine de machines qui sentent la graisse. Ailleurs, deux longues salles pleines de pendules et de régulateurs, ces derniers n'étant que des pendules sans sonnerie.

Museums, streets, seasons, faces

At the Museum of Mankind. Delighted to see Namba again, the goddess of motherhood. Her parrot's beak with the little square of fabric dangling from it and her huge straw cloak make her quite terrifying. I imagined her being carried along in triumph to the sound of the *Marseillaise* or the *Star-Spangled Banner*; that would make her look even odder ... Also inspected the cheerful costume worn somewhere or other for circumcision ceremonies. Farther on there was a marvellous Ubangi drum, two large, flat pieces of wood joined at the top and capped with an extremely delicate buffalo's head that sports very fine, wonderfully curving horns. Seen from the window, over the tops of the Trocadero trees, the Eiffel Tower looked somehow different...

From a room that was all windows, situated on the top floor of a major evening newspaper in the rue du Louvre where I had popped in for a moment, I discovered the most marvellous view I know of the old roofs of Paris: rue Montorgueil, rue d'Aboukir, rue de Cléry ... It was raining hard, and the light was fading amid the great silvery streaks of the downpour. All those seventeenth- and eighteenth-century houses with their caps of brown tiles – how long will they still be there?

At the Museum of Arts and Crafts. A large hall full of machines smelling of grease. Elsewhere, two long rooms full of clocks and regulators, the latter being simply clocks with no striking

Il y en a de toute beauté, depuis le XVIIe siècle jusqu'à 1900, et à cette date, une très charmante horloge appelée horloge mystérieuse qui se compose d'une statuette dorée: une dame très bien sculptée tenant un fil au bout duquel pend une goutte d'eau, bien entendu en cristal, et cette goutte de cristal va et vient. A trois heures et demie, toutes les pendules, à intervalles irréguliers, se sont mises à tinter. Dans ces longues salles où nous étions seuls à l'exception d'un gardien somnolant sur une chaise, ces petites notes d'une pureté admirable, piquant les silences ici et là et plus loin, faisaient un effet bizarre, presque fantastique. On se serait cru dans un conte d'Hoffmann. Du soleil sur les parquets, le temps aboli et pourtant indiqué avec minutie par ces sonneries légères et non concordantes.

La Seine en crue, d'un vert jaunâtre, lourde, majestueuse, couvre les deux berges, et les arches des ponts ont l'air de s'aplatir. Elle est menaçante, orgueilleuse. Je la trouve superbe dans ces moments-là, pleine de colère, une colère souveraine. Le ciel gris foncé fait de Paris une ville toute blanche. Notre-Dame, magnifique de jeunesse.

Boulevard de Clichy, j'ai regardé un vieillard qui faisait travailler, dans la bruine, deux rats blancs et deux fox-terriers à qui la lassitude faisait cligner les yeux. Les rats montaient et descendaient le long des bras de l'homme avec une extrême bonne volonté et une patience en quelque sorte inépuisable. Les chiens coiffés de petits chapeaux tyroliens faisaient le beau autant de fois que cela leur était demandé, mais avec la tristesse que donnent la faim, le froid, la fatigue et la conscience de paraître ridicule. A côté de moi, un gamin observait ces animaux avec gravité. Au bout de quelques minutes, il a tiré de sa poche un gros porte-monnaie usé et, avec un geste où il y avait tout le bon cœur du peuple, il a jeté quelques pièces dans la sébile.

Entre la place Clichy et la place Pigalle, on démolissait les baraques foraines sous une intraitable pluie fine. Je crois que de toutes les grandes villes que j'ai vues, Paris est une des plus tristes, en dépit de cette réputation de gaieté qu'elle a héritée d'une

mechanism. They come in every kind of beauty, from the seventeenth century to 1900, the date of a delightful piece known as a mystery clock. This consists of a gilded statuette, very finely sculpted, of a woman holding a thread with a drop of water on the end, made of glass, of course, and the bead of glass swings to and fro. At half past three all the clocks began to chime at irregular intervals. In those long galleries, where we were alone except for an attendant dozing on a chair, the tiny notes, wonderfully pure, pricking the silences here, there, and everywhere, created an odd, almost eerie effect. It was like being in one of the Tales of Hoffmann. Sunlight on the wooden floors, time done away with yet still meticulously marked by all that delicate, dissonant chiming.

The Seine in flood, grey-green, weighty, majestic, covers both banks, and the arches of the bridges look as if they have been flattened out. The river is haughty, forbidding. I find it magnificent at such times, full of rage, a rage supreme. The dark-grey sky turns Paris quite white. Notre-Dame in youthful splendour.

In the boulevard de Clichy I watched an old man standing in the drizzle, working two white rats and two fox terriers who were blinking with weariness. The rats ran up and down the man's arms with extraordinary willingness and a patience bordering on the inexhaustible. The dogs, who wore little Tyrolean hats, sat up and begged as often as they were required to but with that wretched look that comes from being hungry, cold, tired, and aware of appearing ridiculous. Beside me a small boy stood gazing earnestly at the animals. After some minutes he drew a large, battered purse from his pocket and, with a gesture that encapsulated all the good-heartedness of ordinary folk, tossed a few coins into the bowl.

Between Clichy and Pigalle the stalls were being demolished beneath a persistent fine rain. I think that, of all the big cities I have seen, Paris is one of the saddest, notwithstanding the reputation for

époque heureuse. La misère et la maladie rôdent à toute heure du jour et de la nuit dans les rues de ce morne Montmartre qui brille aux yeux du touriste comme un paradis d'insouciance et de volupté…

Passé en autobus rue Franklin. Il était midi. Un jeune ouvrier est allé vers une fenêtre d'un rez-de-chaussée que décorait un drapeau tricolore sans doute pour le 14 Juillet. Il a pris ce drapeau, en a cassé la hampe sur son genou et en a déchiré l'étoffe; puis il a lancé les débris dans le ruisseau et s'est éloigné d'un pas tranquille. Il eût fait de même avec n'importe quel drapeau, avec cet esprit rebelle qui dort au cœur de chaque Parisien.

Paris dans une brume légère à l'entrée de la nuit, le reflet des lumières dans l'eau, Notre-Dame toute blanche au-delà des ponts, on ne peut rêver un paysage plus ensorceleur.

Au carrefour de la Croix-Rouge, je regardais la rue du Cherche-Midi qui m'a toujours paru avoir quelque chose de magique. Il était cinq heures du soir. Les façades des maisons étaient du haut en bas éclaboussées de lumière, je veux dire qu'on aurait cru que le soleil avait jeté un grand seau de lumière sur ces vieilles demeures et qu'elles en ruisselaient. C'était magnifique et, en même temps, on ne pouvait regarder cela sans éprouver une vague tristesse, la tristesse que donne le soleil.

Boulevard Saint-Germain, non loin de la rue du Bac et presque devant un ministère, sur un banc, un vieillard vêtu d'une veste et d'un pantalon de toile qui semblent faits de pièces cousues les unes aux autres, mais incolores, et de telle sorte qu'on se demande ce qu'il peut rester de la veste et du pantalon originaux qu'on a réparés ainsi; c'est même une sorte de problème philosophique digne d'un spécialiste du Moyen Age. Est-ce le même costume ou en est-ce un autre et à quel moment précis l'un est-il devenu l'autre?

gaiety it has inherited from a happy era. Ceaselessly, day and night, poverty and sickness prowl the dreary Montmartre streets that in the tourist's eyes glitter like a paradise of carefree pleasure ...

In a bus, descending the rue Franklin. It was midday. A young workman walked up to a ground-floor window that was adorned with a French flag, probably for the Fourteenth of July. Seizing the flag, he broke the staff over his knee and shredded the fabric. Then he tossed the bits into the gutter and went calmly on his way. He'd have done the same no matter what the flag had been, with that rebelliousness that lies dormant in the heart of every Parisian.

Paris in a thin mist at nightfall, lights reflected in the water, Notre-Dame all white beyond the bridges – no more bewitching landscape could be conceived.

Standing at the Croix-Rouge crossroads, looking up the rue du Cherche-Midi, which has always held a magical quality in my eyes. The time: five in the evening. The housefronts were spattered with light from top to bottom. I mean to say, it was as if the sun had flung a great bucket of light over those old dwellings, leaving them dripping with it. It was magnificent, and at the same time you could not look at it without experiencing a vague sadness, the sadness bestowed by the sun.

On a bench in the boulevard Saint-Germain, not far from the rue du Bac, almost outside one of the ministries, an old man dressed in a cotton jacket and trousers apparently consisting entirely of patches sewn together, but colourless, in such a way that you wondered what could be left of the original jacket and trousers that had been thus repaired. It was almost a philosophical problem, worthy of the attention of a medievalist; was it the same suit, or was it a different one, and at what precise moment had it become a different one? Anyway, the old man in question had a white beard framing a red,

Quoi qu'il en soit, le vieillard en question a une barbe blanche qui entoure un visage rougeaud et fort sale. Je lui donnerais soixante-dix ans. A côté de lui, sur le banc, un gros réveille-matin, et devant lui, une voiture d'enfant qui donne l'impression d'être passée par un tremblement de terre, mais enfin elle a quatre roues; et dans cette voiture une espèce de berceau au milieu duquel dort un grand chien blanc taché de jaune, sale, inexprimablement serein dans le grand murmure du boulevard.

Ce soir, une légère brume couvrait Paris et les marronniers, éclairés par le dedans par les réverbères, semblaient d'énormes lanternes japonaises...

Au 22 de la rue de l'Echaudé, non loin de Saint-Germain-des-Prés, il y a une porte entrouverte, on la pousse, on découvre un bel escalier du XVIIIe siècle, sombre et mystérieux, avec une cruche d'étain qui orne une niche creusée dans le mur, au repos du premier étage. J'ai regardé longuement la lumière sur ces vieilles marches, je n'arrivais pas à m'en aller...

Un peu plus loin, à l'atelier de Delacroix, place Furstemberg. Le charmant jardin en contrebas où il fait si bon s'asseoir, à l'ombre des arbres, dans le silence où passe la brise, par ce beau jour d'été, à deux pas de l'assourdissant boulevard Saint-Germain. Tout autour, de vieilles maisons aux fenêtres ouvertes, et ces fenêtres sont toutes noires. Des aquarelles de Delacroix, de Huet, de Riesener, de Hugo, partout du rêve. Cette oasis dans notre siècle si tristement dépourvu de poésie. Au-dessus de nos têtes, un ciel d'un bleu léger où flottent des nuages qui ressemblent à de la vapeur.

En fin d'après-midi, je suis entré à l'hôtel Biron pour voir l'exposition de sculpture italienne contemporaine. Dans l'affreuse petite chapelle néo-gothique, un évêque de Manzù fait un effet extra-ordinaire de simplicité majestueuse; il est debout, raide et droit dans son immense cappa magna d'où sort une main; à peine quelques détails çà et là; c'est une grande masse d'une immobilité

very dirty face. I put his age at seventy. On the bench beside him, a large alarm clock; in front of him, a perambulator that looked as if it had survived an earthquake but did at least have four wheels; and in the pram a kind of cradle in which a large, dirty white dog with yellow spots lay sleeping, inexpressibly serene amid the mighty rumble of the boulevard.

This evening a light mist covered Paris, and the chestnut trees, lit from within by the streetlamps, were like huge Japanese lanterns …

At number 22, rue de l'Echaudé, not far from the church of St Germain-des-Près, there is a partly open door that, when you push it open all the way, reveals a fine eighteenth-century staircase, dark and mysterious, with a pewter jug in a niche hollowed out of the wall on the first-floor landing. I gazed for a long while at the light on those ancient stairs, incapable of moving on …

Just past there, Delacroix's studio in the tiny Furstemberg Square. The delightful sunken garden that is so good to sit in, shaded by trees, in the silence cut by the breeze on this fine summer's day, only yards from the deafening boulevard Saint-Germain. All around us, old houses with open windows, and those windows quite black. Watercolours by Delacroix, Huet, Riesener, Hugo, dreams in every direction. This oasis in our century that is so wretchedly devoid of poetry. A pale-blue sky above our heads, with clouds floating in it like puffs of steam.

Late one afternoon I entered Biron House to see the exhibition of contemporary Italian sculpture. In the awful little neo-Gothic chapel a Manzù bishop created an extraordinary effect of majestic simplicity; he stood stiffly upright in his immense *cappa magna*, from which one hand protruded; the odd detail here and there, otherwise this large, thrillingly motionless mass. It was a portrait of Cardinal Lercaro, and it was the Church … Out in the garden, an *Executed Man* lay full-length on the terrace with his hands behind his back, hands that would have set Michelangelo dreaming. Huge,

saisissante. C'est le portrait du cardinal Lercaro et c'est l'Eglise…
Dans le jardin, le *Fusillé*, étendu à terre sur la terrasse, les mains
derrière le dos, des mains à faire rêver Michel-Ange. Enorme et
tragique, la tête belle et jeune… Tout à coup il s'est mis à pleuvoir
très fort et nous avons couru, Eric et moi, sous les marronniers, dans
ces belles allées droites. Sur les pelouses, des sculptures modernes
parfois monstrueuses nous observaient, luisantes, comme des bêtes
de la préhistoire, prêtes à bondir. Un ciel gris, beaucoup de songe
dans tout cela. Il m'a semblé que nous étions dans la Chine de jadis.

A la surface de l'eau le brouillard montait ainsi qu'une vapeur, la
Seine fumait, on voyait dans les profondeurs du ciel noir un air
blanchâtre et opaque; c'était comme si, à l'obscure nuit d'automne,
se substituait une nuit surnaturelle, aussi pâle que l'autre était noire,
mais impénétrable. Elle gagnait les quais, étouffant peu à peu les
lumières. Déjà, on ne voyait plus la rive opposée. Le viaduc de Passy,
avec ses réverbères de couleur, semblait reculer sous la poussée
d'une force irrésistible; la silhouette noire s'effaça d'abord, laissant
dans le vide un long trait rose qui s'évanouit lentement.

Rue de Paradis ce matin pour acheter des verres. Un magasin après
l'autre, tout étincelants de cristal. Baccarat, Saint-Louis, etc. La
belle rue étroite, vivante, puis la rue de Trévise encore plus belle
avec la place ornée d'une fontaine qu'entourent de petits arbres:
que tout cela me parait plaisant et fragile, mais qu'en restera-t-il
dans dix ans? Le ciel gris, l'ondée, c'était le Paris d'autrefois.

Aux Arts et Métiers. Dans ces grandes pièces presque désertes où
tintent des centaines de pendules, le conservateur nous parle d'une
façon passionnante de l'atmosphère légèrement fantastique du
musée à certains moments. A minuit cela est troublant si l'on est
seul. Il y a d'abord le bruit des ressorts des pendules qui s'apprêtent
à sonner les douze coups, puis la multitude des petites notes
égrenées dans le silence.

tragic, the head lovely, youthful … All of a sudden it began to rain very heavily and we ran, Eric and I, under the chestnut trees down those fine, straight paths. On the lawns modern sculptures, some of them monstrous, watched us, gleaming, like prehistoric animals about to pounce. A leaden sky, a very dreamy quality altogether. I felt we were in China, long ago.

From the water's surface fog rose like steam, the Seine smoking, a whitish opacity visible in the depths of the black sky; it was as if the dark autumn night was giving way to a supernatural night, as pale as the other was black, but impenetrable. Little by little it ate up the embankments, stifling the lights one by one. The far bank had already vanished. The Passy viaduct, with its coloured streetlamps, seemed to be retreating under the thrust of some irresistible force; the black silhouette disappeared first, leaving a long pink line that faded slowly.

To the rue de Paradis this morning to buy wine glasses. Shop after shop, all sparkling with crystal. Baccarat, Saint-Louis, other brands. The narrow street beautiful, busy, then the even lovelier rue de Trévise with its square and its pretty fountain set about with little trees: how agreeably fragile it all looks to me, but what will be left of it in ten years' time? The leaden sky, the shower of rain, this was the Paris of old.

At the Arts and Crafts Museum. In those large, almost empty rooms, while hundreds of clocks chimed, the attendant told us fascinating stories about the faintly eerie atmosphere of the museum at certain times. At midnight it can be disturbing if you are on your own. First there is the sound of the springs of the clocks preparing to strike twelve, followed by that intricate ripple of tiny notes in the silence.

There is one particular corner of one of the rooms where, if you are alone, you hear two steps come towards you. The phenomenon,

Dans une des salles se trouve un coin précis où, si l'on est seul, on entend venir vers soi deux pas, phénomène qui s'explique par le jeu des lames du parquet, mais qui n'en est pas moins saisissant. Egalement étrange, l'illusion qu'on a d'un incendie qui s'allume et qui est le reflet d'enseignes lumineuses de la rue frappant les vitrines du musée. On avance et l'on se voit précédé par quelqu'un qui n'est autre que soi-même, toujours par un effet de reflet dans les vitrines. Il y a mieux: dans ce musée, qui eût ravi Hoffmann et Rilke, existe une chambre sourde où se vérifie la précision de certains mécanismes. Le silence y est absolu, un silence que nous ne supportons pas plus d'un instant. Notre silence, si l'on peut dire, n'est que la cessation du bruit, mais dans cette petite pièce règne un silence d'une telle profondeur que personne ne consent à l'endurer plus d'une trentaine de secondes, car non seulement on y entend le bruit de tam-tam que font les battements du cœur, mais le craquement amplifié des os à chaque mouvement. Cela au centre de Paris.

Tout à l'heure à Carnavalet pour voir les salles du bas où se trouvent les vues de Paris à travers les siècles. On en sort avec une impression assez sinistre: ce ne sont que rangées de maisons qui flambent, que gens qu'on colle au mur pour les fusiller, que barricades, que boulets de canon éventrant les palais, émeutes, révolutions, grabuge. J'ai admiré la merveilleuse maquette de Saint-Sulpice de Chalgrin, le Palais-Royal entièrement reproduit avec ses jardins et toutes ses galeries. On regarde tout cela en se penchant dessus, on se fait l'effet d'être un géant, un nouveau Gulliver. Que de colles on pourrait poser même à des professeurs tout le long de la petite histoire de notre ville (où sont passées les momies rapportées d'Egypte, où les a-t-on enterrées, qu'y a-t-il sous la colonne où le génie de la Bastille prend éternellement son vol, où a-t-on détourné le lac souterrain du fantôme de l'Opéra, qui a posé pour la statue de Pierre de Wissant, qui habita le château des Brouillards?) mais on peut toujours être sûr à Paris qu'un amoureux secret connaîtra toutes les réponses.

The rue Cortambert, seen from
the author's apartment window, 1929

The Trocadero being demolished, 1930

Above: A tricycle-carrier, Avenue Wilson, 1934
Below: The rue des Réservoirs, which no longer exists today

Interior view of Julian Green's
Paris apartment, rue Cortambert

A storm over the rue Vaneau, 1974,
taken from Julian Green's apartment window

On the ground floor at the Louvre;
Rodin's 'The Shadow'

Classical statues in the Italian pavilion
during the Colonial Exhibition, 1936

Above: Dalou's monument, place de la Nation
Below: The Bishops' Fountain, St Sulpice

The Monument to Delacroix
in the Luxembourg gardens

Above: The parisian skyline, including the Sacré-Coeur,
seen from the Beaubourg
Below: Bookstalls near Notre-Dame

St Sulpice seen from the rue de Rennes, 1969

Place de la Concorde, 1925

Above: The pont Neuf
Below: The Seine in flood

Above: The Tuileries, winter 1970
Below: Chairs in the Tuileries, 1980

'Strength' by Barye,
in the square on the Ile St Louis

Above: The pont Royal, Notre-Dame and the Institut, 1970
Below: The pont Alexandre III

explicable in terms of play in the floorboards, is none the less startling for that. Another curious illusion is that of a fire flaring up; in fact it is the reflection of neon signs in the street falling on the glass cases of the museum. You walk forward and find someone walking in front of you who is actually yourself – another trick of reflection in the glass cases. Nor is that all: this museum, which would have delighted Hoffmann and Rilke, contains a sound-proofed room used for checking the accuracy of certain mechanisms. In it the silence is total, a silence we cannot bear for more than an instant. Our silence, in a manner of speaking, is simply the cessation of noise, but in that little room there reigns a silence so profound that no one will put up with it for more than thirty seconds or so, for in it you hear not only the tom-tom that is the beating of your heart but the amplified clicking of your bones with every movement. And this is in the middle of Paris.

Just visited the Carnavalet Museum to see the downstairs rooms where they have the views of Paris through the ages. You come away with a pretty sinister impression: nothing but rows of burning houses, people being put up against the wall to be shot, barricades, cannon balls disembowelling palaces, mobs, revolutions, and general mayhem. I admired Chalgrin's wonderful maquette of St Sulpice, the Palais-Royal reproduced *in toto* with its gardens and all its galleries. You look at all this from above, leaning over it, and it makes you feel like a giant, a modern Gulliver. The posers you could set, even for teachers, just by running through the history of our city (what happened to the mummies brought back from Egypt, where were they buried, what lies beneath the column on which the spirit of the Bastille is forever taking wing, where did they divert the Phantom of the Opera's underground lake, who posed for the statue of Pierre de Wissant, who lived in the château des Brouillards?), but in Paris you may always be sure there will be someone, secretly in love with his city, who will know all the answers.

*

Au musée Victor-Hugo. Dans la chambre où se trouve le lit à colonnes il y a, au pied de ce lit, dans une vitrine, le masque mortuaire du vieux fou avec sa barbe qu'on dirait sculptée par le Bernin. Au-dessus de cette vitrine, j'ai vu s'incliner un charmant visage de jeune homme aux cheveux noirs, aux joues brunes. Hugo eût aimé ce contraste. Dehors, sur la place des Vosges, on abattait les ormes. C'était un peu comme si l'on effaçait des milliers de rendez-vous, tendres ou cruels, car ici on pouvait aussi bien s'expliquer par les armes qu'avec des madrigaux...

Promenade autour de la Bourse, dans ces belles vieilles rues un peu sombres, un peu sinistres, avec le souvenir de Chénier, de Lautréamont, de Molière, et de combien d'épisodes de la Terreur ou de 1870. Paris est beau surtout sous un ciel gris. A mes yeux, il a quelque chose de démoralisant sous un ciel trop bleu, qui le rend noir.

Fuyant les Halles qu'on démolit et que les rats quittent à leur tour, me dit-on, pour Rungis, je vais rendre visite à un chanoine de Saint-Eustache. Au bout de l'impasse Saint-Eustache, une porte s'ouvre sur un escalier Renaissance, en pas de vis. Nous montons des marches et des marches, suivons un couloir et débouchons sur le triforium. Là, mes jambes se mettent à trembler. Nous sommes, en effet, à quarante et un mètres au-dessus du pavement de l'église. Je vois les chaises comme des timbres-poste. Un interminable rayon de soleil coupe l'église en deux, passe entre les colonnes comme entre les séquoias dans une forêt américaine. Ce vide énorme, ce silence absolu (l'église est fermée ce lundi de Pâques) me transportent ailleurs.

Rue Cadet, chez un photographe. La maison a un escalier admirable, large et spacieux, avec des ferronneries dignes d'un palais. Beaucoup de maisons tout aussi belles dans ce quartier que j'aime parce qu'il est vivant, et ses maisons sont belles, non par l'ornementation qui en est presque toujours absente, mais par leurs proportions, par

At the Victor Hugo Museum. In the room with the four-poster bed, in a glass case at the foot of the bed, there is a death mask of the old madman, complete with a beard that might be the work of Bernini. I saw, leaning over the case, the charming face of a young man with black hair and brown cheeks. Hugo would have adored the contrast. Outside in the place des Vosges they were felling the elms. It was almost as if they were removing all trace of thousands of rendez-vous, some tender, some cruel – because here people were just as likely to have it out with weapons as with madrigals …

Walked around the Stock Exchange quarter in those lovely, ancient, slightly sombre, slightly sinister streets, thinking of Chénier, Lautréamont, Molière, and so many episodes of the Terror or the Siege. Paris is particularly beautiful beneath a grey sky. To my eye there is something depressing about it beneath too blue a sky, which turns it black.

Avoiding Les Halles, which is being demolished and which I am told the rats, too, are now leaving for Rungis, I go to call on one of the canons of St Eustache. At the bottom of a cul-de-sac, the impasse Saint-Eustache, a door leads to a Renaissance spiral staircase. We climb and climb, pass along a corridor, and come out on the triforium. There my knees start to tremble. We are 135 feet above the floor of the church. I see chairs looking like postage stamps. An endless sunbeam slices the church in two, passing between the columns as between sequoias in an American forest. The vast space and total silence (it is Easter Monday, and the church is closed) have the effect of carrying me away.

At a photographer's in the rue Cadet. The building has a splendid staircase, wide, spacious, and with ironwork that would not be out of place in a palace. Many equally fine houses in this quarter, which I love because it is alive and because its houses are beautiful, not in terms of ornamentation, of which few of them have any, but by

la hauteur des croisées et l'espace entre les croisées. On a perdu le sens de ces choses.

Traversé la Seine à la passerelle de Solférino. Sur les eaux noires du fleuve, des centaines de poissons flottent, le ventre blanc retourné vers le ciel, empoisonnés par les ordures qui polluent notre belle rivière.

Les Tuileries déshonorées par les chevaux de bois, les chemins de fer pour bébés, un grand casino bavarois au fond duquel un groupe de paysans en culotte de cuir yodlent devant quatre clients. Ailleurs des airs de Mozart mugis par une radio assourdissante…

Je suis allé à pied à l'Opéra où je me proposais de m'arrêter un instant au Café de la Paix, mais il est fermé pour transformations. Et je tremble pour ce que cela cache… Sur le boulevard, la foule des jours de congé qui visiblement ne sait que faire de son temps, traînant, faisant la queue devant les cinémas, triste et démoralisante. Je hais le boulevard où je sens le présence d'un ennui presque surnaturel.

Et que dire des entrailles que Beaubourg exhibe avec la satisfaction idiote d'un bébé qui montre son ventre: du troisième étage cependant, une vue admirable sur Paris, mais il faut d'abord passer au milieu de ces gigantesques tuyaux bleu azur et toute cette plomberie qui enguirlande l'extérieur.

Promenade le long de la rue du Cherche-Midi où se voient encore des rangées de maisons aux croisées imposantes, aux persiennes comme des pages d'écriture. C'est ce Paris-là qui est en danger avec le Paris des arbres… En passant pour regarder des meubles, j'ai admiré les vieilles maisons, en particulier le 87 et 89. L'air était doux, la lumière un peu voilée par la brume d'automne, puis il s'est mis doucement à pleuvoir. Debout sur une voiture, un bel ouvrier aux bras nus couvrait les passants d'un regard dédaigneux…

virtue of their proportions, the height of the windows and the space between the windows. We have lost the feeling for these things.

Crossed the Seine by the Solférino footbridge. Hundreds of fish floating on the black water, white bellies turned skyward, poisoned by the filth that pollutes our lovely river.

The Tuileries Gardens disgraced by wooden horses, kiddies' trains, and a large Bavarian casino in which a group of rustics in leather trousers are yodelling to four customers. Somewhere else, Mozart melodies bellow deafeningly from a radio ...

I walk on as far as the Opera House, where I had intended to pay a quick visit to the Café de la Paix. However, it is closed for alterations. I tremble at what that implies ... On the boulevard a typical holiday crowd, obviously with time on its hands, hanging about, queuing outside the cinemas, wretched and depressing. I hate the boulevard, where I sense the presence of an almost super-natural boredom.

And what shall I say of the entrails that the Beaubourg Palace exhibits with the idiotic satisfaction of a toddler baring its stomach? You do, from the third floor, have a marvellous view of Paris, but first you must pass through the middle of those monstrous sky-blue tubes and all the rest of the pipework bedizening the exterior.

Took a stroll along the rue du Cherche-Midi, where you can still see rows of houses with imposing casements and metal shutters like pages of handwriting. That is the Paris now under threat, along with the city of trees ... Passing that way to look at some furniture, I admired the old houses, particularly numbers 87 and 89. The air was mild, the light just veiled by the autumn mist, then a gentle rain began to fall. Up on a lorry, a splendid, bare-armed workman ran a disdainful glance over the passers-by ...

*

Au Louvre. Le Lorrain avec ses ciels couleur de pêche, sa lumière heureuse. De tous les peintres, aucun n'a aussi merveilleusement suggéré ce que peut-être le Pays perdu, le pays d'Ailleurs qui hantera toujours l'humanité. Par les grandes fenêtres qui donnent sur les quais, j'ai regardé Paris sous la pluie, spectacle dont je ne me lasse pas. Puis le soleil s'est mis à briller à travers les gouttes et la ville a pris l'air indéfinissable des lointains dans un des tableaux derrière moi.

Immenses promenades dans Paris. A Cluny, le musée modèle d'aujourd'hui. Disparus les vastes manteaux de velours noir, semés de flammes d'or et d'argent que portaient les chevaliers du Saint-Esprit. Disparu également le diable qui tirait la langue et faisait peur aux religieuses désobéissantes en agitant des chaînes. Là où on l'a mis, il doit rire de son apparente inutilité. Le musée est vide et le gardien qui nous surveille vaguement de salle en salle donne le sentiment d'un prisonnier qui attend l'heure de la visite.

Au Luxembourg, dans le froid. Les arbres constellés de bourgeons blancs et jaunes sous un ciel gris pâle. Les longues lignes parallèles des terrasses, les gros traits noirs que font les rangées d'arbres, tout cela comme dans un dessin qu'à tout jamais grave la mémoire.

Pluie drue et presque incessante sur Paris. Les Tuileries ressemblent à un lac. On y marche dans l'eau. La Seine d'un vert admirable devient majestueuse, couvrant les berges de la rive droite. Ce fleuve aura traversé ma vie comme une force instinctive passe à travers le destin d'un homme. Dans *Epaves*, j'ai essayé de montrer cela par allusion, car autrement comment l'exprimer?

A la Salpêtrière. La chapelle inachevée paraît vide, mais de proportions monumentales. Perfection des lignes et justesse des volumes, mais c'est de Libéral Bruant et de Le Vau, c'est tout dire. Un Christ immense endormi sur sa croix est d'une grandeur de conception

At the Louvre. Claude (we call him 'the Lorrainer') with his peach-coloured skies, his joyful light. Of all painters, none has so wonderfully suggested what the Lost Land might be, the Elsewhere that will forever haunt mankind. Through the large windows that overlook the river I gazed out at Paris in the rain, a sight of which I never tire. Then the sun began to shine through the raindrops and the city took on the indefinable air of the distances in one of the paintings behind me.

Great long walks in Paris. At Cluny, considered today's model museum. Gone are the great cloaks of black velvet spangled with gold and silver flames that were worn by the Knights of the Holy Spirit. Gone, too, is the devil who used to stick out his tongue and frighten recalcitrant nuns by rattling chains. Wherever they have put him, he must laugh at his conspicuous futility. The museum is empty, and the attendant vaguely keeping an eye on us from room to room gives the impression of a prisoner who is waiting for visiting-time.

The Luxembourg Gardens in the cold. Trees studded with white and yellow buds beneath a pale-grey sky. The long parallel lines of the terraces, the fat black lines made by the rows of trees, all as if in a design etched by memory for ever and ever.

Dense, almost incessant rain on Paris. The Tuileries like a lake. People walking in water. The Seine, a wonderful green colour, becoming majestic, covering the lower embankment on the Right Bank. That river will have flowed through my life as an instinctive force informs a man's destiny. I tried in *The Strange River* to show all that by allusion, because how else is one to express it?

At La Salpêtrière. The unfinished chapel looks empty, but its proportions are monumental. Perfection of line and aptness of volume – but then it was built by Libéral Bruant and Le Vau; that says it all.

qui fait battre le cœur. De quelles profondeurs de silence cette croix proteste-t-elle contre l'incrédulité contemporaine …

Sur l'une des portes de ma chambre, le soleil a posé une fenêtre en feu, laquelle se trouve dans la tour Montparnasse. Je vois par la fenêtre de ma chambre cette croisée couleur de rubis dans le soleil couchant, je reste là un moment, puis me retourne, et la voilà un peu plus loin sur une autre porte, elle est d'un rose qui flamboie et si nette que je puis compter les quatre vitres. Je n'ai jamais vu un si beau phénomène de réfraction sauf en montagne.

'Je suis le chemin qui marche à travers Paris, dit la Seine. J'ai emporté bien des images depuis ton enfance et reflété bien des nuages. Je suis changeante, mais comme les hommes: j'ai mes moments de bonheur, l'aube en juin, et mes heures sinistres certains soirs de décembre. Et surtout je suis curieuse, c'est ce que vous appelez des inondations. Nous avons en commun, vous les éternels passants, et moi, l'eau fugitive, de ne jamais revenir en arrière: votre temps, c'est mon espace.

'Quelles lueurs n'ont pas été reflétées par mes eaux! Ma mémoire est un vaste kaléidoscope où tu retrouveras tout ce qui a fait l'histoire de ton siècle: la place de la Concorde en février 1934, quand des femmes vendaient sur des plateaux des billes de métal pour lancer sous les sabots de la cavalerie; les promenades d'amoureux ou d'assassins, comme il y en a dans tes livres; un pape sur le parvis de Notre-Dame pour effacer le souvenir de celui qui n'y était pas venu librement; et tous les feux d'artifice dont ma nuit liquide double les gerbes avant d'en engloutir les sortilèges éteints; et tous les cortèges de mai, ceux de 68, par exemple, qui croyaient à ce que les révolutions du siècle passé n'avaient fait qu'espérer, mais tout recommence et tout se récupère sans cesse chez vous, peuple à palabres; et les premières voitures, hautes et carrées comme des boîtes noires, le long du Cours-la-Reine; et les meubles de l'archevêque qu'on m'a jetés; et les feux de bivouac des Cosaques et des Prussiens; et M. Guillotin

An immense Christ sleeping on his cross is so grandly conceived as to set your heart racing. From what depths of silence does that cross protest against our modern unbelief …

On one of my bedroom doors the sun has laid a fiery window. It is one of the windows in the Montparnasse Tower. I can see the original from my room, coloured ruby-red by the setting sun. I stand looking out for a moment, then turn, and there it is again, a little farther round on another door, a blazing pink and so clear that I can count the four panes. I have never seen such a beautiful refraction phenomenon except in the mountains.

'I am the road running through Paris,' says the Seine. 'I have carried off many images since you were a child and reflected many clouds. I am changeable, but as people are: I have my moments of happiness in the June dawn and my sinister times some December evenings. Above all I am inquisitive – you call it being in flood. We have something in common, you everlasting passers-by and I, the fleeing water, which is that we never go back: your time is my space.

'The lights my surface has reflected! My memory is a great kaleido-scope in which you will find all that has gone to make up the history of your century: the place de la Concorde in February 1934, when women with trays sold metal ball-bearings to throw under the hooves of the cavalry; the walks of lovers or of murderers, as in your books; a pope in the square outside Notre-Dame to erase the memory of the one who had not come there willingly; and all the exploding fireworks that my liquid night mirrors before swallowing up their extinct spells; and all the May Day parades – those of '68, for instance – that believed in what the revolutions of the last century had only held out hope of, but everything starts again, everything is endlessly recycled among this race of interminable talkers; and the first motor cars, high and square like black boxes, bowling along 'Queen's Walk'; and the archbishop's furniture that was tossed into my waters; and the camp fires of Cossacks and Prussians; and Mr

sur sa guillotine, c'était logique; et les sacs encore vivants qu'on balançait par les fenêtres de la tour de Nesles; les petits rois de métal qu'on me lançait du haut du pont au Change contre le mauvais œil, les rixes d'étudiants, les émeutes, les sièges, et la blanche cité qui s'appelait Lutèce quand Attila campait dans les forêts tout autour; car, vois-tu, le temps est aussi rapide en amont qu'en aval.

'Tout ce que tu as vu de ta ville depuis ta jeunesse est vrai, mais les jeunes ne la reconnaîtront pas; cependant, ce sera vite leur tour de décrire une cité que les yeux de leurs enfants ne trouveront plus pareille à leurs propres souvenirs. Et je gage que dans cent ans certains liront avec ravissement qu'il y avait encore à Paris, au XXe siècle, des monstres à quatre roues dans les rues, des escaliers dans les maisons, des tours, des musées, sortes de bric-à-brac où l'on entassait des images peintes et toutes sortes de choses; à moins que Paris ne soit devenu, comme dans l'imagination de Jules Verne, un lieu sur une carte marine où des requins et des tortues géantes nageront parmi les pierres glauques, et moi-même, une trace un peu plus sombre dans le limon de cette nouvelle Atlantide!

'Quoi qu'il en soit, je demeurerai toujours à ma place invisible; songe que je traverse trop de Paris imaginaires, celui de *Maldoror*, des *Misérables*, d'*Epaves* … mais pour tous les corps que vos romans ont noyés dans mon lit, j'entends encore les cris réels que mes flots ont avalés, j'ai toutes les preuves qu'on a cachées dans mon sein depuis le Moyen Age, j'ai les secrets des suicidés, et si tu veux, comme les autres, savoir ce que je pense vraiment de Paris, je te conseille de regarder avec ton cœur le sourire mystérieux de l'*inconnue de la Seine* …'

Guillotin on his guillotine, of course; and the sacks, still alive, that were flung out of the windows of the Nesles Tower; the little metal kings that folk used to throw down from the pont au Change to ward off the evil eye, the student brawls, the riots, the sieges, and the white city that was known as Lutetia when Attila camped in the forests all around; time, you see, goes as fast upstream as down.

'Everything you have seen of your city since your youth is true, though young people will not recognize it; nevertheless, it will soon be their turn to describe a city that their children, in turn, will find no longer conforms to their memories. And I guarantee that in a hundred years' time people will be delighted to read that there were still, in twentieth-century Paris, four-wheeled monsters in the streets, staircases in the houses, towers, museums like junkshops where people amassed painted pictures and all manner of objects; unless, as in the imagination of Jules Verne, Paris has become a spot on a chart, where sharks and giant turtles swim amid the sea-green stones and I am a slightly darker line winding through the silt of a new Atlantis!

'Be that as it may, I shall still occupy my invisible place; remember, I flow through too many imaginary Parises, the Paris of *Maldoror*, the Paris of *Les Misérables*, the Paris of your own *The Strange River* ... For all the bodies your novels have drowned in my bed, however, I can still hear the real cries that my waves have engulfed, I hold all the evidence that has been concealed in my bosom since the Middle Ages, I possess the secrets of the suicides, and if, like the others, you want to know what I really think of Paris, my advice is to gaze with your heart upon the mysterious smile of the *woman of the Seine* ...'

Paris enchanté

Paris m'a hanté à un tel point toute ma vie que plusieurs de mes personnages romanesques ont hérité de moi cette fascination et ce goût des promenades solitaires et aventureuses à travers la capitale. Encore aujourd'hui, il me suffit de suivre l'un ou l'autre d'entre eux pour retrouver à travers eux et comme redoublé par leur propre rêverie le trouble ou l'enchantement d'un lieu où je reviens par hasard.

Ainsi le passage du Caire où Fabien attendait l'aventure, je ne peux m'y trouver, même par une après-midi ensoleillée, sans que pour moi le temps ne soit *autre*: il est nocturne et la pluie tombe. Je l'ai en quelque sorte fixé dans mon souvenir et j'entends malgré moi les pas mesurés qui viennent de l'autre côté du passage pour aggraver l'inquiétude de celui qui attend. Vais-je me retourner? 'Si j'étais toi, murmure une voix intérieure, je ne le ferais pas, car tu sais bien que tout cela est du rêve et de l'invention.'

Mais si, pour voir, je fermais les yeux une seconde, si Paris, celui que j'ai imaginé, devenait le vrai, si le passage du Caire était désert, qu'il fasse sombre, que la pluie crépite sur les verrières opaques? Les vitrines luisent sinistrement... Ne vais-je pas entendre les pas tranquilles s'approcher et la voix qui donnait à mon héros le pouvoir d'émigrer de corps en corps prononcer insidieusement le sésame: 'Si j'étais vous...'

Enchanted Paris

Paris has so haunted me all my life that several of the characters in my novels inherited my fascination and my liking for lone, adventurous walks through the streets of the capital. Even today I need only follow one or another of them to rediscover, through them and as if intensified by their own reverie, the turmoil or the enchantment of a particular place I happen to return to.

I can never find myself in the passage du Caire, for example, where Fabien awaited adventure, even on a sunny afternoon, without the time and the weather being, so far as I am concerned, *otherwise*: it is night, and raining. I have somehow fixed it in my memory, and despite myself I hear the measured steps coming from the other leg of the passage to heighten the anxiety of the person waiting. Shall I turn round? 'If I were you, Julian,' a voice inside me murmurs, 'I shouldn't, for, as you very well know, that is all dreaming and invention.'

But what if, to see, I shut my eyes for a second; what if Paris, the one I had imagined, became the real one; what if the passage du Caire was deserted, and it was dark, with the rain pattering down on the opaque glass above my head? The shop windows gleam sinisterly … Shall I not hear the quiet steps approach and the voice that gave my hero the power to migrate from body to body pronounce the insidious open sesame: 'If I were you …'

Cris perdus

Parmi tous les *cris* qui se sont tus, qui se souvient 'du mouron pour les p'tits oiseaux'? Quelle âme désabusée inventa cet air aux modulations d'une tendresse poignante? C'est une plainte si douce qu'on dirait qu'elle renonce à se faire entendre, le gémissement d'une nostalgie secrète. On l'entendait dans certaines rues parisiennes, la petite phrase unie qui traversait la grosse rumeur du marché; elle ne se mêlait ni aux vociférations des maraîchers ni au roulement des voitures, mais côtoyait tout ce bruit, comme une étrangère passe à côté d'une foule.

Et la femme qui proférait ce chant mystérieux marchait toujours entourée d'une grande solitude, quand même on la bousculait. Son visage gardait une expression de surhumaine indifférence. Elle tenait à la main une poignée d'épis pesants et dorés qu'elle faisait voir d'un geste absent, comme pourrait faire une Cérès en exil qui montrerait, sans espoir d'être comprise, le symbole d'une religion oubliée. A son bras, un panier large et profond contenait l'inutile marchandise, car pourquoi nourrir des bêtes qui ne savent que chanter? Parfois elle tirait sur sa poitrine un châle dont un pan glissait de son épaule, et sa voix lointaine avait la douceur de certaines voix de folles ou de somnambules qui parlent d'on ne sait quoi de nocturne et d'apaisé. Aussi n'allaient vers elle que de petites vieilles aux jupes démodées et qui par un geste prudent et maniéré tiraient de leur sac une pièce de métal. Avec quelle grâce l'épi leur était tendu qu'elles serraient dans leurs maigres doigts. On croyait presque surprendre un rite à voir la femme au châle

98

Lost cries

Among all the street cries now heard no more, who remembers 'chickweed for the little birds'? What disabused soul composed that tune with its tenderly poignant modulations? It was a lament so soft it seemed not to want to be heard, the sigh of a secret longing. You heard it in certain streets of Paris, the plain little phrase cutting through the great hubbub of the market; it blended neither with the shouts of the stall-holders nor with the roar of the traffic but skirted all that noise as a foreigner will walk round a crowd.

And the woman who used to pour out that mysterious song was always surrounded by a vast solitude, even when she was being jostled by people. Her face wore an expression of superhuman indifference. In her hand she held a sheaf of heavy, golden ears, displaying them with a vacant gesture such as an exiled Ceres might use to exhibit, with no hope of being understood, the symbol of a forgotten religion. A wide, deep basket on her arm contained the useless merchandise, for what is the point of feeding animals who can do nothing but sing? One flap of her shawl kept slipping off her shoulder, and every now and then she would tug it across her bosom; her faraway voice had the sweetness of certain madwomen's voices, or those of sleepwalkers speaking of something nocturnal, assuaged. So no one went near her but little old ladies in no longer fashionable skirts, who with careful, affected gestures took a coin from their bags. How graciously the ear was offered to them, which they then clutched in their skinny fingers. It was almost as if you had stumbled across some rite, seeing the woman with the shawl

glissant placer un brin de mouron dans cette main lourdement veinée, et cette pièce offerte en échange prenait tout à coup un air d'antiquité extrême et un sens propitiatoire.

slipping off one shoulder place a strand of chickweed in the heavily veined hand, and the coin tendered in exchange suddenly took on an air of immense antiquity, assuming a propitiatory connotation.

Paysage parisien

Nous savons bien que Paris est beau, mais les peintres nous le redisent avec toute l'autorité de leur génie et l'on demeure muet devant une ville que Manet, Degas, Monet et tant d'autres nous donnent, si différente de ce que nous voyons et pourtant si réelle. Que dire devant les Tuileries sous le ciel d'avril de Pissarro ou les quais en hiver, sous un ciel de neige de Gauguin ou dans le crépuscule rose de Lebourg? La bouche se tait, les yeux seuls parlent.

Il y a dans un paysage parisien quelque chose d'aussi parfaitement indéfinissable que l'expression d'un visage humain. Bien des peintres ont essayé de saisir cette expression, mais peu y ont réussi, quelque soin qu'ils aient mis à l'observer. Ce don de la ressemblance appliqué à une ville comme Paris est très particulier. Dans un tableau qu'on pourrait dire non ressemblant, il se peut que tous les arbres soient à leur place et les maisons rendues avec une exactitude scrupuleuse, mais il manque quelque chose, et ce quelque chose, c'est Paris même, c'est la présence invisible de Paris, l'esprit qui anime la lumière et l'ombre du feuillage sur les pierres. Si l'on regarde ensuite la vue des boulevards de Pissarro, ou la vue de Montmartre que Van Gogh a peinte de son atelier, on éprouve une espèce de choc intérieur, le choc que seule donne la vérité, quand elle attire la lumière et la brume et le ciel dans un ou deux mètres carrés de toile et les y fait vivre à jamais.

On peut dire que Paris a été la ville des impressionnistes. Or, ce qui frappe d'abord dans l'œuvre de ces peintres, c'est son énorme

Parisian landscape

We know, of course, that Paris is beautiful, but painters tell us so over again with all the authority of their genius, and we find ourselves struck dumb by a city that Manet, Degas, Monet, and so many others place before us, so different from what we see and yet so real. What can one say, faced with the Tuileries Gardens under Pissarro's April sky, or the Seine embankment in winter beneath a snow-laden sky by Gauguin or in Lebourg's roseate dusk? Lips are silent; only eyes have the power of speech.

There is something in a Parisian landscape that is as wholly indefinable as the expression on a person's face. Many painters have tried to capture that expression, but few have succeeded, however painstaking their observation. This gift of likeness applied to a city such as Paris is very special. In a painting that might be judged a poor likeness, it may be that, while all the trees are in the right places and the houses are depicted with scrupulous accuracy, something is missing, and that something is Paris itself, the invisible presence of Paris, the spirit that informs the light and shade of foliage on the stones. If you then look at Pissarro's view of the boulevards, or the view of Montmartre that Van Gogh painted from his studio, you feel a kind of shock inside you, the shock that only the truth administers when it draws the light and the mist and the sky into one or two square metres of canvas and makes them live there for ever.

Paris may be said to have been the city of the Impressionists. Now, the first thing that strikes you about the work of those painters is how enormously simple it is. It has the simplicity of a field of oats

simplicité. Elle est simple comme un champ d'avoine et de coquelicots sous un ciel d'août, simple comme une allée de tilleuls dans une petite ville de province; et elle est libre comme l'air, car elle s'est échappée de la prison des formules comme l'air passe à travers les barreaux. Elle a planté son chevalet en plein vent. Et les peintres lâchés avec leurs pinceaux et leurs pliants sur les bords de la Seine ou dans les rues de Paris nous ont montré une ville d'une sérénité radieuse, une ville où le ciel donnait exactement l'illusion de participer à tous les jeux du jour. Nous sommes loin de la cité de pierre et de marbre de Baudelaire, mais les poètes ont dans le cœur la vision tragique de leurs désirs. Nos peintres, eux, ne voyaient pas ce paysage obscur, ils faisaient des ombres avec des couleurs claires et regardaient comme des enfants les jardins, les averses et les rues animées, et sous les grands nuages blancs qui traversent d'un bout à l'autre leurs ciels, ils nous rendent un Paris heureux, la ville de la lumière.

and poppies beneath an autumn sky, the simplicity of an avenue of lime trees in a small provincial town; also it is as free as air, having escaped from the prison of formulas as the air passes between prison bars. It set up its easel in the open. And the painters let loose with their brushes and their campstools on the banks of the Seine or in the streets of Paris showed us a city radiant in its serenity, a light, bright city, even beneath a stormy sky, a city in which the sky gave the precise illusion of joining in all the day's games. We are a long way from Baudelaire's city of stone and marble, but poets carry in their hearts the tragic vision of their desires. They did not see that dark landscape, our painters; they made shadows with bright colours and looked with the eyes of children upon gardens, rainshowers, and busy streets; and beneath the great white clouds that traverse their skies from end to end they restore to us a happy Paris, the city of light.

Ecoute, bûcheron ...

Chaque année, je vois les arbres disparaître. On a beau dire qu'on en replante, on n'en retrouve jamais le même nombre et c'est toujours une quantité moindre qui tend de nouveau ses jeunes bras vers le soleil ou secoue sa chevelure dans le vent.

Paris est la seule ville où l'on traite ainsi nos frères les arbres; ni Berlin ni Londres, pour ne citer que des villes civilisées, ne montrent une telle méconnaissance de la nature. Chaque année, sous les prétextes les plus divers, nos avenues présentent un cortège digne des 'malheurs de la guerre' et les mutilés dressent leurs moignons au-dessus de l'indifférence des voitures en grande partie coupables de cette maladroite extermination. Si comme le dit Aristote les arbres sont des personnes qui rêvent, que pense l'arbre de ses bourreaux? Je ne veux pas jouer à lui donner une voix, car il a pour lui le silence des amoureux, les jeux d'enfants, les rêveries du solitaire et le peuple libre et sans contrainte, je veux parler des oiseaux. Alors font-ils le poids ces soi-disant experts du taillage, de l'émondage, de tous ces noms variés dont ils déguisent leurs méfaits? De l'asphalte et de la poussière, c'est ce qu'ils veulent, sans idée de ce qu'est Paris et ses jardins vus du ciel. Imaginent-ils que les promeneurs disparaîtront avec le siècle et que les arbres ne survivront pas? Depuis la préhistoire ils ont grandi avec la race humaine, comme parallèlement, et quand l'homme s'est dressé sur ses membres inférieurs, la plante a grandi qui rampait encore au temps des grands monstres antédiluviens, comme s'il lui fallait protéger celui qui était né pour être le roi de la nature. De quoi

Hear me, wood-cutter . . .

Year by year I see the trees disappearing. It's no good people saying they replant: you never find the same number. Each time there are fewer of them to raise their young arms towards the sun once again or shake their tresses in the wind.

Paris is the only city in which our brothers the trees are treated in this way; neither Berlin nor London, to mention only civilized cities, displays such ignorance of nature. Each year, on a wide variety of pretexts, our avenues present a spectacle worthy of *The Disasters of War*, and the mutilated victims lift their stumps above the indifference of the motor cars that are largely to blame for this clumsy extermination. If, as Aristotle says, trees are people day-dreaming, what does the tree think of its executioners? I have no desire to play at giving it a voice, since it has on its side the silence of lovers, children's games, the musings of the solitary, and the free folk that knows no constraint, by which I mean the birds. Are they any match for all that, these so-called experts at pruning and trimming and all the other words they use to disguise their misdeeds? Asphalt and dust are what they want, with no conception of what Paris and its gardens look like from the sky. Do they suppose the strollers will disappear with the century and the trees not survive? Since prehistoric times they have grown with the human race – alongside it, so to speak – and when man stood up on his hind legs, the plant that at the time of the great antediluvian monsters had still been a creeper grew tall as if to protect him who was born to be the king of nature. What are they kings of, these

sont-ils les rois, ces gens qui coupent et taillent, pour qui l'arbre c'est du bois et qui méritent toujours l'invective de Ronsard au bûcheron de la forêt de Gastines?

> *Combien de feux, de fers, de morts et de détresses,*
> *Mérites-tu, méchant…*

people who lop and prune, for whom a tree is simply timber, and who still merit Ronsard's imprecations upon the wood-cutter of Gastines Forest?

> *How many fires, fetters, deaths, and sufferings,*
> *Do you deserve, you wretch …*

La ville sur la ville

Dans toutes les villes d'Europe, comme il y a la ville des hommes, il y a la ville des statues. Je ne veux pas parler de celles qu'on voit sur les places, dans les jardins, à hauteur du regard sur les façades, et qui sont un peu comme les sentinelles de ce monde de pierre, de bronze ou de marbre, épiant de près en quelque sorte nos démarches incompréhensibles comme le sont pour l'homme ordinaire l'agitation des insectes.

Il existe sur les toits, aux flancs ou au fronton des églises, des palais ou des bâtiments officiels que nous légua le XIXe siècle, un monde parallèle qui défie les sautes d'humeur du temps et considère le soleil comme les morts doivent regarder la gloire. Beaucoup de ces allégories, car là où elles ont été placées il s'agit plus d'idées que de personnages mémorables, ne sont visibles d'en bas que partiellement. Pour un Apollon qui lève sans fin sa lyre au-dessus du monde minéral des avenues de l'Opéra, comme s'il voulait l'éloigner du flot hideux des véhicules, ou pour un Ganymède enlevé par l'aigle d'une compagnie d'assurances – à moins que ce ne soit un phénix – au-dessus de la tranchée bleuie par les gaz d'échappement du boulevard Haussmann, que de vertus cachées qu'on ne surprend que des lucarnes d'un septième sans ascenseur ou, si le hasard vous a incité à venir avec des jumelles, dans un petit bureau sous les combles du Louvre ou sur la terrasse d'un grand magasin. Que voient-elles, ces 'Saisons' éternellement printanières, ces 'Tempérance', ces 'Justice'? A quoi rêvent ces 'Génies' méconnus, ces 'Théologies' idéales, tout ce capharnaüm

The city above the city

In every European city, there is the city of the people and there is the city of the statues. I don't mean the ones you see in squares and gardens and at eye level on the façades of buildings, which seem almost to be standing guard over that world of stone and bronze and marble, keeping, as it were, a close watch on our movements – surely as baffling as the average man finds the teeming of insects.

Up on the roofs, and on the sides or fronts of churches and palaces or of the public buildings bequeathed to us by the nineteenth century, there exists a parallel world, defying the mood swings of time and eyeing the sun as the dead must gaze upon glory. Many of these allegories (for up where they have been placed we find ourselves dealing more with ideas than with memorable people) are only partially visible from below. For one Apollo endlessly holding his lyre aloft above the mineral world of the avenues that meet at the Opera House, as if to keep it clear of the hideous stream of vehicles, or one Ganymede carried off by an insurance company's eagle – unless it's a phoenix, is it? – above the cutting of the boulevard Haussmann, blue with exhaust fumes, how many secret virtues are there that you come upon only from the dormers of some seventh floor without a lift or, if chance prompted you to bring your binoculars, in a little study up in the attic of the Louvre or on the terrace of a department store. What can they see, those forever vernal 'Seasons', those figures representing 'Temperance' or 'Justice'? What do they think about, those unrecognized 'Geniuses' who (in French) represent engineering, those ideal 'Theologies',

abstrait dont on a cru se débarrasser dans des recoins inaccessibles aux hommes d'en bas? Et que font-elles, ces statues, le soir, quand l'ombre égalise la terre, par les nuits de brume de novembre, par les nuits sans lune ou, au contraire, quand la lune de mai laque les toits de la ville comme les lames d'une mer sombre?

J'imagine que la distance n'existe pas pour elles, pour les évêques mitrés du fronton de Saint-Roch, pour les chimères et les réprouvés de Notre-Dame, pour les têtes aux yeux fixes qui surmontent une gare d'Orsay vidée de son hôtel et de ses guichets comme un coquillage abandonné par son bernard-l'ermite, et pour le grand ange Jugendstil de la rue Réaumur. Songent-elles aussi à leurs disparus, quand par mode les hommes deviennent iconoclastes, quand une guerre transforme Chappe et son télégraphe, La Fontaine, Dolet, Gambetta et combien d'amours de bronze en canons? Ce que l'homme crée, l'homme le détruit avec dirait-on le même plaisir, comme s'il avait finalement peur du monde sorti de son cerveau et de ses mains, Pygmalion effrayé que sa Galathée ne lui échappe et se transforme en Vénus d'Ille, à l'envers de ce que Dieu fit avec cette statue vivante qu'était Adam, quand il lui donna un second corps.

all that abstract junk that it was thought could be tucked away in nooks and crannies out of the reach of the people below? And what do they get up to in the evening, those statues, when darkness levels out the earth, on misty November nights, on moonless nights or, on the contrary, when the May moon lacquers the roofs of the city like the waves of some dark sea?

I suppose distance does not exist for them, for the mitred bishops on the façade of St Roch, for the chimeras and reprobates of Notre-Dame, for the heads with staring eyes that top the deserted Orsay station, now stripped of its hotel and its ticket offices like a shell vacated by its hermit crab, and for the huge Jugendstil angel of the rue Réaumur. Do they, too, remember their dead, when fashion has moved men to become iconoclasts or when a war turns Chappe with his telegraph, La Fontaine, Dolet, Gambetta and innumerable bronze cupids into guns? That which man creates, man destroys with, it would seem, equal pleasure. It is as if he was ultimately frightened of the world that has emerged from his head and from his hands, Pygmalion afraid lest his Galatea escape from him and turn into the Venus of Ille in a reversal of what God did with the living statue that was Adam when he gave him a second body.

Inventaire du futur

Que sera Paris demain? J'y pensais en regardant le long de la Seine dans la brume la gloire des bourgeons qui couvrent les arbres d'un voile léger. Paris est d'une beauté qui m'inquiète par moment parce que je la sens fragile, menacée. Menacée surtout par nos urbanistes. Quel jeune architecte nous donnera enfin la cité du futur, une belle ville capable de séduire ceux qui viendront, comme nous avons été ensorcelés par le Paris façonné peu à peu par les siècles. Est-ce trop de rêver un visionnaire qui soit le poète de l'espace et non plus l'un de ces organisateurs de la *vie en laid* pour paraphraser Baudelaire, un de ces traqueurs de l'espace perdu qui font des immeubles modernes des cubes sans grâce, pleins du bruit et de la fureur des télévisions et des canalisations des voisins...

Il y a d'inévitables destructions, on ne peut pas éternellement gémir sur ce qui fut. Mais le temps aurait dû nous apprendre à ne plus protéger sottement ce qui était fait pour ne pas durer, toutes ces maisons construites pour cent ans et qu'on rafistole dans certains coins du Marais ou du faubourg Saint-Antoine.

Au seuil du XXIe siècle, nous vivons avec les idées les plus arriérées, particulièrement dans la façon de bâtir nos villes. Il n'est pas question d'abolir le passé, mais d'en user comme d'une mémoire, et l'inventaire que fera le futur, c'est d'abord celui de tout ce que les générations nous ont offert de beauté depuis la première pierre taillée par l'homme.

Inventory of the future

What will Paris be like tomorrow? The thought was in my mind as, strolling beside the Seine in the mist, I contemplated the glory of the buds that covered the trees with a delicate veil. Paris possesses a beauty that alarms me at times because I feel it is fragile, under threat. Mainly from our town planners. Which young architect is at last going to give us the city of the future, a fine city capable of appealing to the generations to come as we have been enchanted by the Paris that has been fashioned slowly by the centuries? Is it too much to dream of a visionary who will be the poet of space and no longer one of those organizers of a *life uglified*, to paraphrase Baudelaire, one of those beaters of wasted space who erect modern apartment buildings as graceless cubes, full of the sound and fury of the neighbours' television sets and plumbing facilities...

A certain amount of destruction is inevitable; we cannot be forever moaning about what is gone. But time should have taught us not to go on stupidly protecting what was made not to last, all those houses put up a hundred years ago and now being patched up in parts of the Marais and around the faubourg Saint-Antoine.

On the threshold of the twenty-first century, we are living with the most antiquated ideas, particularly as regards how to build cities. It is not a question of getting rid of the past but rather one of using it like a memory, and the inventory that the future draws up will be mainly that of all the beauty that has been given to us down the generations since the first stone cut by man.

L'espace et la nature, il faut toujours en revenir là, et l'architecture moderne ne peut se satisfaire de principes étriqués qui font reconstruire Paris par petits bouts, ici les Halles, là Montparnasse ou le XVe, sans vue d'ensemble, sans l'imagination de *demain*. Il y a eu de tout temps des visionnaires, et le 'rêve de l'architecte' de Thomas Cole rejoint les rêves de Soane, de Loos ou de Klenze d'un Londres, d'une Vienne ou d'un Munich idéaux. Jefferson alla plus loin, il construisit ce qu'il avait rêvé, l'Université de Virginie où j'ai terminé mes études. Mais les grands créateurs français, les Ledoux, les Boullée, les Le Corbusier, n'ont pas eu le bonheur de voir leurs visions devenir réelles, et ce qu'ils ont pu réaliser, nos édiles se sont ingéniés à y mettre bon ordre. Les programmes de Boullée, ses projets de basilique, de mausolée, de théâtre, les plans de Ledoux pour des hôtels, des places publiques, des quartiers d'artisans, sont presque toujours restés à l'état de dessins qu'on admire dans des cartons de musée. Et notre siècle montre la même méfiance. Pour une Brasilia, que de Sarcelles!

Depuis que je suis né dans le XVIIe, près de la porte des Ternes, après des guerres, des années d'exil, et même après chacun des voyages qui m'ont conduit presque partout où je voulais aller, j'ai retrouvé ma ville natale avec le même élan d'admiration chaque fois. Je la vois changer. On dirait que les responsables contemplent l'avenir, leur longue-vue tournée dans le mauvais sens. Que leur importe la beauté des ciels, les arbres, tout ce qui met le bonheur dans les yeux des passants...

Dans mille ans, il y aura peut-être un homme, debout comme moi derrière la vitre d'une croisée et qui regardera comme je regarde à présent ce paysage de maisons derrière des arbres et ce ciel de pluie printanière. J'essaie de me figurer que j'ai franchi ce grand espace de temps et que je suis cet homme. A quoi pense-t-il? Est-il heureux? Se demande-t-il quelquefois pourquoi il est sur terre et pourquoi à telle époque et non à telle autre? Que croit-il? Que voit-il? Cette curiosité qu'il éveille en moi, d'autres l'ont eue à notre égard qui se sont endormis dans les temps où Lutèce

Space and nature – it always comes back to that. And modern architecture cannot content itself with narrow-minded principles such as are having Paris rebuilt in bits and pieces, Les Halles here, Montparnasse or the fifteenth district there, with no overall view, no thought of *tomorrow*. There have always been visionaries, and the 'architect's dream' of Thomas Cole matches the dreams of Soane, Loos, or Klenze of an ideal London, Vienna, or Munich. Jefferson went further: he built what he had dreamed – the University of Virginia, where I completed my studies. The great French creators, however, people like Ledoux, Boullée, Le Corbusier, were not lucky enough to see their visions become reality, and what they did manage to build our city fathers contrived to put to rights. Boullée's *programmes* and basilica, mausoleum, and theatre projects, Ledoux's plans for town houses, public places, and districts for craft-tradesmen hardly ever progressed further than the drawings that we admire in museum boxes. And our century exhibits the same suspicion. How many Sarcelles for one Brazilia!

Since the time when I was born in the seventeenth district, near the porte des Ternes, after wars and the years of exile, even after each of the trips that have taken me almost everywhere I wished to go, I have returned to my native city to feel the same rush of wonder every time. I can see it changing. You would think those responsible were contemplating the future with their telescopes turned round the wrong way. What is the beauty of skies to them, or trees, or all the things that put gladness in the eyes of passers-by …

A thousand years from now, perhaps, a man will stand as I am standing behind a windowpane and look as I am looking at this landscape of houses behind trees and this sky scattering spring rain. I try to imagine having crossed that great space of time and being that man. What is he thinking about? Is he happy? Does he sometimes wonder what he is doing on this earth and why at one period rather than another? What does he believe? What can he see? This same curiosity that he arouses in me, others had about us before they passed away in the days when Lutetia was first emerging from

sortait à peine de sa boue. Ici peut-être, à l'endroit même où je me tiens, un Barbare a rêvé aux hommes de l'avenir. Et moi, je songe à ce Paris futur, élevé sur l'espace qui est le nôtre, et où le béton brut, le verre, l'acier, et peut-être d'autres matériaux inconnus encore, seront les éléments d'une beauté sans fin.

the mud. Maybe on this very spot where I am standing a Barbarian mused about the men that were to come. And here am I, dreaming of that Paris of the future, raised up on the space that is now ours, where shuttered concrete, glass, steel, and possibly other materials as yet unknown will be the ingredients of a limitless beauty.

Notes

<table>
<tr><td>11</td><td>The Marais, now the third and fourth arrondissements, is one of the most ancient parts of Paris, with many fine old buildings.</td></tr>
</table>

11   The Marais, now the third and fourth *arrondissements*, is one of the most ancient parts of Paris, with many fine old buildings.

    The fifth district includes the Sorbonne, the university that goes back to a foundation of 1253.

19   Jean-Paul Marat (1743–93) was one of the most fiery journalists of the French Revolution. He was assassinated (in his bath) by Charlotte Corday, a great-niece of the dramatist Pierre Corneille.

    Théophile Gautier (1811–72), French poet, novelist, and journalist to whom Baudelaire dedicated *Les Fleurs du mal*.

23   François Mansart or Mansard (1598–1666), the great protagonist of French classicism in architecture.

25   Philippe Auguste was one of the greatest of the early French kings. The many achievements of his reign (1180–1223) included the construction of a fortified wall around Paris.

29   Marie Bashkirtseff (1860–84) was the author of an intimate diary covering almost half her short life.

    The painter Edouard Manet (1832–83) is also buried in Passy cemetery.

    Benjamin Franklin (1706–90) is honoured in Paris as America's first ambassador to France (1776–85).

49   The Knights of the Holy Sepulchre were members of an order revived by Pope Alexander VI towards the end of the fifteenth century for the purpose of guarding the tomb of Christ.

57   Isidore Ducasse (1846–70), the self-styled 'comte de Lautréamont', was the author of the hallucinatory *Chants de Maldoror*, one of the greatest poems in all French literature.

63   The pont des Saints-Pères, virtually a continuation of the rue des Saints-Pères, is what Parisians call the pont du Carrousel.

Dr Samuel Johnson (1709–84): 'No, sir, when a man is tired of London, he is tired of life; for there is in London all that life can afford' (Boswell's *Life of Johnson*, 20 September 1777).

65   The Barberini notoriously demolished the Circus Maximus in Rome to make way for their palace.

67   Charles VII, Joan of Arc's monarch, reigned 1422–61.

69   Thomas à Kempis (1380–1471) is generally believed to have been the author of the *Imitation of Christ*.

71   The Trocadero Palace, built by Davioud and Bourdais for the 1878 Paris Exhibition, was demolished and replaced by the present Palais de Chaillot (which consists of two 'wings' without a body; see above, page 29) for the 1937 Paris Exhibition.

73   The Tuileries Palace burned down as a result of the civil conflict between the *Communards* and the *Versaillais* during the siege of Paris in 1871.

81   The painter Eugène Delacroix (1798–1863) and the cabinetmaker Jean-Henri Riesener (1734–1806) both lived and worked in the place Furstemberg. Paul Huet (1803–69) and Victor-Marie Hugo (1802–85) are represented by drawings and watercolours in the Delacroix Collection.

Biron House is the home of the Rodin Museum.

Giacomo Manzù (1908–91), Italian sculptor.

The Executed Man is the work of the Italian sculptor Pericle Fazzini (1913–87).

83   Jean-Eric Green is the author's son.

85   The architect Francois Chalgrin (1739–1811) also designed the Arc de Triomphe for Napoleon.

The mummies brought back from Egypt (by Napoleon) were first placed in the Museum of Antiquities, then buried beneath the column in the place de la Bastille, and finally laid to rest in Père Lachaise cemetery.

Beneath the column in the place de la Bastille lies a small circular chamber which for a time held the bodies of those killed during the revolution of June 1848.

The underground lake celebrated in Gaston Leroux's novel *Le Fantôme de l'Opéra* is now only vestigially present beneath the Opera House, most of it having been diverted to a site under the nearby rue de Provence, where it forms part of the city's sewer network.

Rodin's model for Pierre de Wissant, one of the 'burghers of Calais', was a popular Comédie-Française actor called Coquelin *cadet* (to distinguish him from his even better-known elder brother, Coquelin *aîné*, creator of the role of Cyrano de Bergerac).

The romantically named château des Brouillards, an eighteenth-century folly in Montmartre, was for a while home to the writer Gérard de Nerval (1808–55) (but not, contrary to popular belief, to the painter Renoir, who merely inhabited the outbuildings).

87　The poet André Chénier (1762–94), the writer Isidore Ducasse (1846–70), who assumed the name Lautréamont (see note to p.57), and the dramatist Jean-Baptiste Poquelin (1622–73), who assumed the name Molière, all lived in this part of Paris.

Rungis, in the southern suburbs of Paris near the Porte de Gentilly, is the present site of the city's fruit and vegetable market, which moved there from Les Halles in the early 1970s.

The canon of St Eustache is the composer Père Emile Martin.

91　*The Strange River*, a translation of Julian Green's 1931 novel *Epaves* by Vivian Holland, was published in 1932 by Heinemann (UK) and Harper (USA).

93　The Montparnasse Tower, a 58-storey block erected in 1974, dominates the southern skyline of Paris.

93–4　What the Seine witnessed in the place de la Concorde in February 1934 was a popular riot directed against the Chamber of Deputies and the government. The first pope referred to is John Paul II, who visited Paris in 1980; the other is Pius VII, brought to Paris as a prisoner in 1810 following Napoleon's invasion of the Papal States. The archbishop's furniture was thrown into the river during the siege of Paris in 1870–71, and the campfires of the Cossacks and the Prussians were seen in 1814 and 1871 respectively.

95　Joseph-Ignace Guillotin (1738–1814), a professor of anatomy and member of the Estates General summoned in 1789, was the proposer rather than the inventor of the device that came to bear his

name (it was designed by the secretary of the College of Surgeons and built by a German mechanic named Schmidt).

The Nesles Tower (also spelled Nesle), which stood on the site now occupied by the Institut de France, was associated with the legendary crimes of Marguerite de Bourgogne (*c.* 1290–1315) and inspired Alexandre Dumas *père* to write his historical drama *La Tour de Nesle*.

The Jules Verne novel alluded to is *Une ville flottante*.

The woman of the Seine was a woman whose body was recovered from the river some time around the middle of the nineteenth century, wearing an expression of such perfect serenity that a plaster cast was taken of her face. You can still buy copies of her death mask in gift shops today.

97   Fabien is the hero of Julian Green's 1947 novel *Si j'étais vous*, which was translated into English by John McEwan as *If I were you* and published by Eyre & Spottiswoode in 1949.

107–9   'Hear me, wood-cutter' translates the opening words of, and 'How many fires …' is an extract from, Pierre de Ronsard's moving poem *Contre les bûcherons de la forêt de Gastine* (*Elégies* XXIV), written in protest against the destruction of a well-loved forest (the name of which is sometimes written 'Gastine'). The extract is translated into English by Arthur Boyars.

113   The Venus of Ille, a bronze statue in a *nouvelle* by Prosper Mérimée (*La Vénus d'Ille*, 1837), is inadvertently brought to life by (and subsequently appears to have occasioned the sinister death of) a young man who had slipped his bride's ring onto its finger.

115   In 'Le mauvais vitrier', a piece in Baudelaire's *Petits poèmes en prose* (1869), the narrator upbraids an itinerant glazier for not, in a poor district, peddling coloured glass 'pour voir la vie en beau'.

117   Sarcelles, a disastrous 'new town' in the northern suburbs of Paris, is afflicted by all the usual problems of poverty, violence, crime, and racial tension.

Bibliographic Details

'J'ai bien des fois revé d'écrire …' was written in 1945 and first published in *Oeuvres complètes* (Pléiade).

'Passy' was written in 1943 and published in *Pour la Victoire*, New York, 1943.

'Saint-Julien-le-Pauvre' was written in America in 1943 and first published in the *Oeuvres complètes*.

'Les hauteurs du seizième' was written in 1943 and published in *Pour la Victoire*.

'Une ville secrète' was first published in the *Oeuvres complètes*.

'Le Palais-Royal' was written in 1944 and first published in the *Oeuvres complètes*.

'A Notre-Dame' was written in 1946 and first published in the *Oeuvres complètes*.

'Paris des escaliers' was first published in 1946 in *Plaisir de France*.

'Le Val-de-Grâce': part of this text appears in the *Oeuvres complètes*; the rest was published here, in *Paris*, for the first time in 1983.

'La vilaine école' was first published in the *Oeuvres complètes*.

'Le cloître des Billettes' was first published in *Le Figaro* in 1946.

'Le Trocadéro parle', an extract from the *Journal*, was published here, in *Paris*, for the first time in 1983.

'Musées, rues, saisons, visages': extracts from the *Journal*, written at various times and many of them published here, in *Paris*, for the first time in 1983.

'Paris enchanté' was first published here, in *Paris*, in 1983.

'Cris perdus' was first published in the *Oeuvres complètes*.

'Paysage parisien' was first published here, in *Paris*, in 1983.

'Ecoute, bûcheron …' was first published here, in *Paris*, in 1983.

Bibliographic Details

'La ville sur la ville' was first published here, in *Paris*, in 1983.
'Inventaire du futur' was first published here, in *Paris*, in 1983.

PENGUIN MODERN CLASSICS

A SPY IN THE HOUSE OF LOVE
ANAÏS NIN

'Her sense of woman is unique … she excites male readers and incites female readers' *The New York Times*

Sabina is a firebird blazing through 1950s New York: she is a woman daring to enjoy the sexual licence that men have always known. Wearing extravagant outfits and playing dangerous games of desire, she deliberately avoids commitment, gripped by the pursuit of pleasure for its own sake.

In *A Spy in the House of Love*, Anaïs Nin expressed her individual vision of feminine sexuality with a ferocious dramatic force. Through Sabina's affairs with four men, she lays bare all the duplicity and fragmentation of self involved in the search for love.

Penguin Modern Classics

WIND, SAND AND STARS
ANTOINE DE SAINT-EXUPÉRY

'A Conrad of the air … Like Conrad, Saint-Exupéry is a poet of action'
André Maurois

In 1926 Antoine de Saint-Exupéry (author of the classic *The Little Prince*) began flying for the pioneering airline Latécoère – later known as Aéropostale – opening up the first mail routes across the Sahara and the Andes. *Wind, Sand and Stars* (1939) is drawn from this experience.

Interweaving stories of encounters with the nomadic Arabs and other adventures into a rich autobiographical narrative, it has its climax in the extraordinary story of Saint-Exupéry's crash in the Libyan Desert in 1936, and his miraculous survival.

Translated with an Introduction by William Rees

PENGUIN MODERN CLASSICS

THE PLAGUE
ALBERT CAMUS

'Camus's great novel rings truer than ever; a fireball in the night of complacency'
Tony Judt

The townspeople of Oran are in the grip of a deadly plague, which condemns its
victims to a swift and horrifying death. Fear, isolation and claustrophobia follow
as they are forced into quarantine, each responding in their own way to the lethal
bacillus: some resign themselves to fate, some seek blame and a few, like Dr
Rieux, resist the terror.

An immediate triumph when it was published in 1947, Camus' novel is in part
an allegory for France's suffering under the Nazi occupation, and also a story of
bravery and determination against the precariousness of human existence.

'An impressive new translation … of this matchless fable of fear, courage and
cowardice' *Independent*

Translated by Robin Buss
With an Introduction by Tony Judt

WINNER OF THE NOBEL PRIZE FOR LITERATURE

PENGUIN MODERN CLASSICS

THE REBEL
ALBERT CAMUS

'One of the great humanist manifestos on the twentieth century' *The Times*

Camus described this brilliant essay on the nature of human revolt as 'an attempt to understand the time I live in'. Published in 1951, it expresses his horror at the events of a period which 'within fifty years uproots, enslaves or kills seventy million human beings'. Hope for the future, he argues, lies in revolt, which unlike revolution is a spontaneous response to injustice and a chance to achieve change without giving up individual or collective freedom. *The Rebel* created an irreconcilable rift between Camus and his friend Jean-Paul Sartre who bitterly attacked Camus for his criticism of communism.

'*The Rebel* should be read as a daring, emotional and intellectual biography' Olivier Todd

Translated by Anthony Bower
With an Introduction by Olivier Todd

WINNER OF THE NOBEL PRIZE FOR LITERATURE

Contemporary ... Provocative ... Outrageous ...
Prophetic ... Groundbreaking ... Funny ... Disturbing ...
Different ... Moving ... Revolutionary ... Inspiring ...
Subversive ... Life-changing ...

What makes a modern classic?

At Penguin Classics our mission has always been to make the best
books ever written available to everyone. And that also means
constantly redefining and refreshing exactly what makes a 'classic'.
That's where Modern Classics come in. Since 1961 they have been an
organic, ever-growing and ever-evolving list of books from the last
hundred (or so) years that we believe will continue to be read over and
over again.

They could be books that have inspired political dissent, such as
Animal Farm. Some, like *Lolita* or *A Clockwork Orange*, may have
caused shock and outrage. Many have led to great films, from *In Cold
Blood* to *One Flew Over the Cuckoo's Nest*. They have broken down
barriers – whether social, sexual, or, in the case of *Ulysses*, the
boundaries of language itself. And they might – like *Goldfinger* or
Scoop – just be pure classic escapism. Whatever the reason, Penguin
Modern Classics continue to inspire, entertain and enlighten millions
of readers everywhere.

'No publisher has had more influence on reading habits than Penguin'
Independent

'Penguins provided a crash course in world literature'
Guardian

The best books ever written

P E N G U I N CLASSICS

SINCE 1946

Find out more at www.penguinclassics.com